AF556144

圖書在版編目（CIP）數據

鵬背集 / 胡曉明著．— 北京：國家圖書館出版社，2022.12

ISBN 978-7-5013-7391-8

Ⅰ．①鵬…　Ⅱ．①胡…　Ⅲ．①詩集—中國—當代　Ⅳ．① I227

中國版本圖書館 CIP 數據核字（2021）第 242576 號

鵬背集

胡曉明 著

MADIRA

Parag A. Shastry is a storyteller, spirits strategist, and innovation leader with a deep interest in mixology and India's diverse drinking cultures. Over the past decade, he has become a prominent voice in the country's craft liquor movement, known for exploring alcohol not just as a beverage, but as a cultural marker shaped by memory, ritual, and community.

As General Manager–Innovation and Marketing at Diageo India, Parag helped create new-to-the-world spirits and brands inspired by India's sensory and cultural landscape. His work sits at the intersection of heritage and modern consumer behaviour, giving him a nuanced understanding of how India's drinking identity is evolving across bars, homes, and emerging craft ecosystems.

His connection to this subject is deeply personal. Having grown up across small-town India–from the Nimad, Chambal, and Malwa regions of Madhya Pradesh to the tribal districts of Gujarat, Vidarbha in Maharashtra, and the North Bengal tri-border area–Parag witnessed firsthand the local brews, indigenous rituals, and community drinking customs that quietly shape India's relationship with alcohol. These experiences shaped his belief that a drink is never only about what is poured into a glass, but also the stories, traditions, and meanings that surround it.

In *Madira: India's Forgotten Spirits and Cocktail Revival*, he brings together cultural storytelling, sustainable practices, and contemporary cocktail ideas to offer an India-first perspective on spirits–one where the narrative behind a drink holds equal importance as the drink itself. His work blends professional insight with cultural immersion, offering a rare lens into how tradition and innovation can coexist behind the bar.

Through this book, Parag hopes to inspire bartenders, enthusiasts, and curious readers to rediscover India's flavours and stories, and to view cocktails not merely as drinks, but as expressions of place, memory, and identity.

MADIRA

INDIA'S FORGOTTEN SPIRITS AND COCKTAIL REVIVAL

PARAG A. SHASTRY

First published by
Rupa Publications India Pvt. Ltd 2026
161-B/4, Gulmohar House,
Yusuf Sarai Community Centre,
New Delhi 110049

Sales centres:
Bengaluru Chennai
Hyderabad Kolkata Mumbai

P-ISBN: 978-93-7003-126-5
E-ISBN: 978-93-7003-977-3

First impression 2026

10 9 8 7 6 5 4 3 2 1

Printed in India

Contents

Foreword

In the world of spirits and stories, few books manage to do what *Madira* accomplishes so effortlessly—bridge the gap between memory and modernity, between heritage and innovation.

India has always been a land of layered flavours. Our kitchens hum with complexity, our rituals are infused with symbolism, and our celebrations overflow with abundance. Yet, for reasons both historical and systemic, our drinking traditions were long overshadowed. While the West polished its wine culture and Japan elevated its whiskies, India's indigenous alcohol—rooted in botanical wisdom and crafted through generations—remained under-acknowledged, even within our own borders.

Until now.

Madira is not merely a book. It is a reclamation. A beautifully distilled journey through India's forgotten spirits, brought back to life through a lens that is both scholarly and spirited. With every chapter, the reader is invited not just to sip, but to reflect—to taste the legacy behind mahua, to understand the cultural rhythms of toddy, to imagine the warmth of Arrack under royal chandeliers or rural skies.

What makes this work truly singular is the way it merges craftsmanship with context. Each cocktail isn't just a recipe—it's a revelation. You begin to see how turmeric isn't just a spice, but a mood; how kokum isn't just tangy, but ancestral.

There's a reverence here that elevates mixology into cultural preservation.

In an age where sustainability is a buzzword, *Madira* quietly reminds us that India has always practiced zero-waste living, long before the phrase was fashionable. The ingredients showcased, the upcycled methods shared, the hyper-local approach to flavour—all of it echoes a tradition that is deeply Indian and deeply relevant.

Parag A. Shastry brings to this book not only industry experience but a rare sense of storytelling and cultural immersion. He writes like someone who has lived both the ritual and the revival. There's a sincerity that makes this more than a manual—it's a movement in a bottle.

If you've ever wondered what India might taste like when poured into a glass, balanced with spice and soul, *Madira* is your answer.

Read it. Drink from it. Share it. And most importantly—remember it.

Vikram Damodaran
Chief Innovation Officer, Diageo India

Who This Book Is For

This book is not just for bartenders.

It's for anyone who's ever paused to inhale the scent of a fresh lime before slicing it. For those who believe that every celebration has a flavour, and that memory can be stirred—not just recalled.

Yes, *Madira* offers recipes that professional mixologists will appreciate—but it is equally a book for:

- **Curious at-home cocktail enthusiasts** who want to experiment with flavours beyond the familiar, and serve something that sparks a story.
- **Cultural explorers and food writers** looking to uncover the secret lives of Indian ingredients, rituals, and indigenous brews.
- **Story lovers and design romantics** who find joy in the unexpected places where taste, tradition, and memory collide.

This book is born out of the deeply immersive experiences I've had across India—from tribal mahua brews shared in forest clearings, to coconut toddy tapped at sunrise on coastal backwaters, to wedding feasts where a single homemade drink held generations of ritual in its making. I've been fortunate to walk through forgotten villages, festival kitchens, roadside taverns, and luxury hotel bars—gathering not just ingredients, but emotions, rituals, and stories along the way.

Madira can be read with or without a shaker in hand. Each cocktail is a doorway into a region, a season, a feeling. The stories behind the spirits, the ingredients, and the techniques are as essential as the drinks themselves.

Whether you are sipping solo, hosting friends, researching the roots of Indian flavour, or simply wandering through the soul of a country through its drinks—you'll find something here that resonates.

This isn't just a cocktail book.

It's a storyteller's guide. A ritual map. A love letter to India, poured one sip at a time.

What This Book Is About

This isn't just a book of cocktail recipes. It's a journey through time, flavour, and tradition. It's a celebration of the drinks we once savoured, the ingredients we took for granted, and the techniques that were lost in the tide of modern drinking culture.

Inside these pages, you won't just find instructions on how to mix a cocktail—you'll find **stories**. Stories that bring to life the culture, history, and rituals that make Indian drinking traditions so unique.

There are **101 uniquely Indian cocktails** waiting for you, each crafted with **local spirits, fragrant spices, and ingredients that have been part of our kitchens and celebrations for centuries.**

Some of these drinks are inspired by **royal feasts and ancient rituals**, while others are reinventions of **classic cocktails with a distinctly Indian soul**. Every recipe has a story—**some rooted in history, some inspired by tradition, and some simply born out of the joy of experimentation.**

This book isn't just about following recipes; it's about understanding how **a single sip can capture the essence of a region, a festival, or even a forgotten moment in time.**

At its heart, **this is a book about rediscovery**—about bringing back the flavours we once celebrated, mixing them with modern creativity, and raising a glass to everything that makes Indian mixology bold, inventive, and exciting.

And, of course, it's about **having fun.** Because drinking isn't just about what's in the glass—it's about the experience, the storytelling, and the shared moments that make each cocktail special.

So before we begin, pour yourself something good. It doesn't have to be fancy—just something that makes you feel at home.

Because this book? **It's a toast to India's cocktails—past, present, and future.**

A Taste of What's to Come

Every great drink starts with a story. This one begins in Banaras...

But before we dive into the structure, ingredients, or rituals of Indian cocktails, let me tell you a story.

A small one. But one that captures everything this book is about.

Back in the late 1800s, when the British still believed they had 'civilized taste' and an upper hand in all things refined, an English officer found himself wandering through the ghats of Banaras. The city was known for its spiritual wisdom, bustling markets, and deeply rooted traditions—including its secret potions.

One evening, after a particularly long day of attempting (and failing) to understand the complex web of Indian spices, the officer stumbled into a small, dimly lit tavern tucked between two ancient temples. The place smelled of roasted fennel, aged molasses, and something floral in the air.

Behind the counter stood Kallu Bhaiya, a local bartender who had seen enough foreigners wincing at the strength of Indian spirits.

The officer, wanting to assert his dominance over 'exotic' flavours, leaned in smugly and declared: 'I'll have something refined. None of your local muddy concoctions. A proper drink, like a Brandy Sour!'

Kallu Bhaiya nodded, hiding a mischievous grin. He reached behind the counter and pulled out an old copper pot that held a rich, golden liquid. He mixed it with a squeeze of freshly plucked Gondhoraj lemon, a swirl of jaggery syrup, and finished it with a sprinkle of toasted cumin powder.

The drink had an intoxicating aroma—earthy, bright, and layered with complexity.

The officer took a sip, expecting something harsh, but instead, his eyes widened in surprise.

'By Jove! This...this is smoother than anything I've ever tasted!' He gulped it down, nodding with approval.

Kallu Bhaiya leaned in. 'That, sahib, is what we call a Banarasi Toddy—mahua-based, naturally sweet, balanced with citrus and spice. No imported brandy, no foreign syrups. Just pure Indian craft.'

The officer blinked, suddenly realizing that all his years of London club drinks had never introduced him to a flavour this bold, this alive.

From that night onward, he never ordered a Brandy Sour again. Instead, he kept coming back for Kallu Bhaiya's Banarasi Toddy, learning the flavours, the traditions, and finally, that Indian bartenders weren't just making drinks—they were making history in a glass.

Kallu Bhaiya wasn't just serving drinks. He was reclaiming pride, tradition, and storytelling—one pour at a time. And that spirit is exactly what flows through every recipe you'll find in this book.

You'll meet many more storytellers like him in the pages ahead—some real, some remembered, some reimagined.

Each one with their own rhythm. Each one with their own pour.

So let's begin—not with techniques, but with tradition. Not with a recipe, but with a ritual.

Chapter 0

Madira

India's Forgotten Spirits and the Cocktail Revival before the First Pour

This story starts not with the clink of ice or the splash of spirits, but with silence—the quiet absence of something precious. It begins with what was once celebrated and then suppressed, cherished and then nearly forgotten.

Before cocktails were shaken and stirred, Indian drinking was ceremonial—rooted deeply in ritual, identity, and reverence. Our spirits weren't merely beverages; they were invocations. They carried memory, heritage, and a sense of belonging.

This chapter revisits that silence, retracing the journey from pride through erasure, and lays the foundation for revival. To truly appreciate what we're rediscovering, we must first remember a time before whiskey touched our shores.

Once Upon a Time, There Was No Whiskey

Long before mixers lined bars and imported liquors arrived by the crate, India spoke a different drinking language—

distinctly regional, profoundly ritualistic, and quietly confident.

In royal courts, drinks steeped in saffron were poured from silver goblets, reflecting status and sophistication. Along southern shores, toddy was tapped fresh at dawn, passed hand to hand with the easy intimacy of village gossip. Across tribal heartlands, flowers, fruits, and grains fermented quietly without recipes, guided solely by intuition.

In Arunachal, rice beer wasn't just a drink; it marked life's celebrations. In Odisha, fermented brews honoured seasonal harvests, deeply tying community to land. And in Chhattisgarh, mahua wasn't merely a spirit–it was sustenance, devotion, livelihood, and song.

We were never casual drinkers. Our traditions were intentional, layered, and inventive. Each beverage carried meaning, context, and cultural pride. They were not commodities; they were communal offerings–each pour an act of storytelling.

The Great Erasure

Then came the British–and with them, a new gospel: if it wasn't bottled in Europe, it wasn't worth drinking. They did not just import spirits, they imported judgement. Local brews were criminalized, taxed, banned. Indigenous distilleries shut down. Toddy tappers became outlaws. What was once sacred was now 'illicit'.

Over generations, we learned to look down on our own spirits. Mahua became the 'poor man's drink'. Feni was relegated to holiday souvenirs. Arrack was pushed into the shadows.

In their place came Scotch, gin, and rum–symbols of sophistication. We weren't just robbed of our drinks–we were robbed of our pride in drinking.

The Comeback: A Cocktail Renaissance

History moves in circles, and eventually, it brings us home.

Today, India is experiencing a quiet yet powerful renaissance—reclaiming the cocktail culture that was always ours. From the stylish backbars of Bandra to hidden speakeasies in Goa, a new generation of bartenders and drinkers is rediscovering spirits that had once been pushed aside.

Mahua is now being cold-distilled and elegantly bottled like a fine fragrance. Goan feni ages gracefully in teak barrels, making its way into sophisticated Negronis. Ingredients once dismissed as merely 'local'—Gondhoraj lime, kokum, tulsi, jaggery, tamarind—have become the soulful heart of the modern Indian cocktail.

We're no longer looking outward for inspiration. We're defining our own tradition, creating a distinctly Indian cocktail canon—rich in heritage, bold in creativity, and authentic in every pour.

Why This Book Now

Madira is more than a collection of cocktail recipes; it's a living document of revival.

Think of it as part drinker's diary, part cultural exploration, and entirely a celebration of the senses. Inside, you'll find cocktails inspired by temple offerings, roadside stalls, royal kitchens, hidden forests, and festive gatherings. Each recipe is a doorway to an experience—some deeply personal, others carefully researched, many directly witnessed, and a few joyfully imagined.

Yet every cocktail within these pages is bound by a single conviction: India's indigenous spirits deserve to be recognized, respected, and rediscovered.

This is not merely about bringing forgotten cocktails back into fashion. It's about restoring their rightful context—rooted in our rituals, memories, and shared history.

So, here's to everything we once overlooked: the fermented, the forgotten, the fragrant. Here's to reclaiming our rituals, redefining flavour, and celebrating the quiet revolution stirred into every thoughtfully crafted cocktail.

The bar is now open.

And this time, the drinks—and the stories they tell—belong to us.

Raising the Glass Again

Understanding our past empowers us to act consciously. The revival ahead is not just nostalgic longing; it's a deliberate reclamation of heritage. Each cocktail you'll meet isn't simply a beverage—it's an intentional blend of tradition and innovation, history and modernity.

As you turn these pages, remember: we aren't just mixing drinks. We're mixing identity, restoring dignity, and pouring India's spirit back into every glass.

Chapter 1

The Indian Cocktail Renaissance

Why It's Happening Now | The Quiet Revolution

Behind every cultural shift stands a group of quiet revolutionaries. India's cocktail revival is no different. Bartenders, distillers, and discerning drinkers across India are subtly rewriting rules—embracing craft over convenience, authenticity over imitation, and local heritage over imported trends.

This chapter uncovers the roots of this revival. Why is it happening now? Why are Indian spirits reclaiming their rightful place on global shelves and local menus? And why does each thoughtful pour today feel like an act of gentle rebellion?

The Rise of Indian Craft Spirits

For decades, India's liquor landscape was defined by uniformity—generic whiskeys, mass-produced rums, and artificially flavoured mixers. Craft spirits were unknown, and quality was measured only by the brand's imported pedigree.

Today, a new wave of Indian distillers has reshaped the scene, elevating local spirits to global acclaim. Indian single malts–brands like Amrut, Paul John, and Godawan–have begun to outshine Scotch whiskies in international competitions, proving that India's diverse climates and innovative craftsmanship can create whiskies of unparalleled complexity.

Feni and mahua, previously dismissed as rustic 'village liquors', now find their way into sophisticated cocktail lists worldwide. Distillers bottle mahua like fine perfumes, while Goan feni matures in teak barrels, lending depth to elegant Negronis.

Even the gin scene has witnessed an unprecedented transformation. Indian-made gins like Hapusa, Stranger and Sons, and Greater Than–infused with native botanicals like Himalayan juniper, turmeric and mango leaf–have captured global attention and local pride.

This isn't mere innovation. It's a return to roots, a reclamation of flavours steeped in our soil for generations.

From Predictable to Playful: The Cocktail Revolution

Not long ago, Indian drinking meant predictability–whiskey with soda or rum with cola. Occasionally vodka with juice. The palette was limited, the creativity non-existent, and drinking experiences, repetitive and uninspired.

Then came millennials and Gen Z, bringing with them curiosity, creativity, and demand for deeper experiences. These new drinkers did not want passive consumption–they wanted storytelling in their glasses. Suddenly, the same old spirits weren't enough. They demanded cocktails that spoke of their origin, drinks that used local ingredients, infused with fresh, authentic flavours.

Indian bars responded in kind–crafting cocktails with

kokum, jaggery, tamarind, and Gondhoraj lime, each sip narrating a story of place and identity. Bartenders infused spirits with spices, herbs, and fruits once relegated only to kitchens, reimagining traditional flavours into contemporary experiences.

This generation isn't just drinking—they are curating their drinking experiences, choosing flavour and authenticity over convenience. Indian cocktails, finally, have begun to reclaim their narrative.

Sustainable by Nature: The Indian Way of Drinking

The West may now champion 'zero-waste cocktails', but for India, this ethos isn't novel—it's foundational. The Indian kitchen has always been a place of innovation, where leftover ingredients find new life in ingenious ways.

Citrus peels dried into spice blends, tea infusions, or caramelized for garnish;
Fruit pulp transformed into syrups or fermented bases for homemade liqueurs;
Overripe bananas blended into creamy rum punches and spiced whiskey sours;
Discarded tamarind seeds roasted and steeped into smoky infusions, evoking street-side coolers;
Leftover rice fermented overnight into mild, naturally alcoholic rice beer, enjoyed traditionally before a day's labour.

Indian cocktails, like Indian cooking, inherently honour the philosophy of waste nothing. Every ingredient, every scrap, finds renewed purpose and deeper meaning.

Sustainability, thus, isn't an imported concept—it's intrinsic. As the global bar community moves toward eco-conscious drinking, India's timeless practices offer lessons in genuine sustainability—rooted in necessity, tradition, and respect for resources.

The Return of Ritual

Indian drinking traditions were never solitary—they have always thrived on community, shared celebrations, and collective joy. Unlike Western drinking culture, which often leans toward individual indulgence, Indian rituals prioritize gathering, storytelling, and shared moments.

Today's cocktail movement seamlessly integrates into these cultural rhythms. Instead of simply pouring spirits into glasses, we shake, stir, infuse, and create. Each drink is crafted consciously, as much a ritual as the festivals and ceremonies they accompany.

We're not just reinventing drinks—we're reclaiming our cultural heritage. In this revival, each cocktail honours history, celebrates locality, and reconnects us with the communal joy of drinking.

THE FINAL SIP: INDIA'S COCKTAIL FUTURE

This renaissance isn't fleeting—it's here to stay, growing steadily from exclusive urban bars to homes across India. Cocktails, once restricted to upscale lounges in Mumbai, Delhi, or Bangalore, are now vibrant fixtures in casual weekend gatherings, family celebrations, and house parties everywhere.

The best part? This is only the beginning.

We are stepping beyond mass-produced, one-dimensional drinks into a universe of bold, nuanced, and regionally inspired flavours. For the first time, India isn't merely consuming global trends—it's shaping them.

The pages ahead are not just filled with recipes—they

are journeys. Each cocktail you encounter is a crafted experience, a sip of our collective identity, a celebration of our diverse and vibrant culture.

It's time to reclaim what has always belonged to us.

The future of cocktails is distinctly, unapologetically Indian. And it begins here.

Theory into Practice

Now that we've explored the 'why' behind India's cocktail revolution, it's time to delve deeper into the 'how'. The next chapter isn't simply about making drinks—it's about crafting experiences. The cocktails that follow blend intention with imagination, method with mindfulness.

Ready your shaker, gather your ingredients, and open your senses—not just your hands, but your heart.

Let's pour meaning into every glass.

Chapter 2

The Art of Sustainable Mixology

India's Cocktail Revolution with a Conscience | The Mindful Pour

In India, a cocktail doesn't begin in a glass—it begins in the soil, the season, and the senses. Ingredients aren't merely chosen; they're invited. To craft a cocktail here means to listen carefully—to nature's rhythms, ancestral traditions, and intuitive creativity.

This chapter delves into the essence of cocktails made with consciousness—mixes crafted with respect for the environment, in harmony with the seasons, and rooted deeply in sustainability. Welcome to the mindful pour: where every sip respects its source.

A Country That Mixes by Instinct

Cocktail-making in India is not borrowed flair—it's inherited intuition. Long before the term 'mixology' entered our vocabulary, we stirred palm toddy with jaggery, infused mahua flowers with spices, and sipped herbal brews under banyan trees.

Unlike Western practices—with their imported spirits, precise ratios, and stainless-steel shakers—our approach is seasonal, sensory, and spiritual. A truly Indian cocktail doesn't start at the bar; it originates in the kitchen, in gardens, or in the comforting memory of a grandmother simmering herbs on a winter morning.

Summer drinks cool the core, infused with raw mangoes and fresh mint. Winter cocktails offer warmth, wrapped with jaggery, clove, or the golden whisper of saffron.

Before we pour our first drink, let's anchor ourselves in the Madira philosophy of conscious crafting.

The Sacred Cycle of the Sustainable Sip

Inspired by the Five Elements. Guided by Intention.

In India, a cocktail isn't assembled; it's invoked—balanced carefully with the five classical elements: Earth, Water, Fire, Air, and Ether. This is not just a method. It's a sacred ritual.

- **Prithvi (Earth):** Use what grows around you. Raw mango, turmeric, jamun, or tender coconut—seasonal, local, soulful.
  The soil speaks through flavour. Listen.
- **Jal (Water):** Balance and cleanse. Water brings clarity, purity, connection.
  Even a splash of water carries memory.
- **Agni (Fire):** Transform the forgotten. Toast peels, reduce syrups, roast spices. Turn waste into wonder.
  Fire doesn't destroy—it reinvents.
- **Vayu (Air):** Let flavours rise again. Foam your kokum, smoke your cinnamon, spritz citrus zest.
  What lingers in the air, lingers in the heart.

- **Akash (Ether):** Create with intention. Akash is imagination and energy—the invisible essence making a cocktail unforgettable.
  A true cocktail lives in the space between technique and soul.

The Building Blocks of a Perfect Sustainable Cocktail

Every Indian cocktail combines five essentials, not in rigid ratios but in flowing harmony:

- **Spirit:** Think beyond vodka and gin—reach for mahua, feni, or toddy
- **Sweetener:** Jaggery syrup, honey, or ripe fruit pulp
- **Sour/Bitter:** Gondhoraj lime, tamarind, raw mango, sour plum
- **Mixer:** Coconut water, spiced soda, or tulsi infusion
- **Garnish:** Edible flowers, toasted seeds, or citrus ash—never plastic swizzles

It's not about impressing the palate—it's about moving the soul.

India's Seasons and Their Signature Sips

India doesn't sip uniformly through the year. Our cocktails shift with monsoons, mango harvests, and winds of seasonal change. Just as farmers watch the sky, Indian bartenders watch the seasons—not just for flavour but for truth.

Summer (March–June): Cooling and Reviving

- Ingredients: Raw mango, kokum, rose, mint, Gondhoraj lime, coconut water
- Ideas: Aam panna mojito, kokum tequila cooler, coconut gin fizz

Monsoon (July–September): Spiced and Grounding

- Ingredients: Ginger, lemongrass, saffron, jaggery, tamarind, star anise
- Ideas: Ginger whiskey smash, tamarind margarita, jaggery hot toddy

Autumn (October–November): Fruity and Festive

- Ingredients: Pomegranate, figs, nutmeg, tulsi, cinnamon, honey
- Ideas: Pomegranate old-fashioned, tulsi gin sour, fig and rum punch

Winter (December–February): Bold and Warming

- Ingredients: Clove, saffron, mahua, dried fruit, black pepper
- Ideas: Smoked clove Manhattan, saffron whiskey punch, hot mahua toddy

The Story of the Pledge: My Friend Rohit from Parel

A few years ago, in a quiet, sunlit heritage building in Parel, I met my friend Rohit—a rising voice in India's cocktail movement. His bar emphasized restraint, elegance, and deep understanding of ingredients.

That evening, Rohit stirred a cocktail unlike anything I had tasted: ghee-washed single malt, tulsi distillate, raw forest honey, and saffron. Layered, aromatic, deeply Indian—not just in flavour, but philosophy.

'What inspired it?' I asked.

'My mother,' he smiled. 'She never cooked without context. Each chai was crafted for the season, mood, moment—no shortcuts, no waste.' He paused thoughtfully. 'She told me, "The most thoughtful thing you can serve is something remembering its source." That guides me.'

Hours passed between stories and sips, and that evening, we shaped a quiet pact—not as bartenders but as custodians of taste:

- Look to our kitchens first.
- Use every gift from nature, even what's not Instagram-friendly.
- Invent instead of discarding.
- Compost what we can't pour.
- Drink not just for taste, but for the story.

Great cocktails aren't just crafted—they're cared for, from root to rim, earth to ether.

Sustainable mixology isn't sacrifice; it's respect. For the land, season, and spirit around every glass. We don't just drink; we invoke, remember, and celebrate.

When done right, nothing is wasted—not a peel, a spice, nor a moment.

This isn't just how we drink. It's how we live. This is *Madira*.

The Glass and the Gift

Drinking sustainably isn't only ethical—it's elegant. You've now learned not just recipes, but how to rethink your relationship with ingredients, waste, and tradition.

As you turn to the recipes ahead, carry forward this conscious craftsmanship. Remember, sustainability isn't a garnish—it's the very glass we drink from.

Stir mindfully, sip respectfully, and waste nothing.

Chapter 3

Let Your Glass Tell a Story

How to use this book | A Journey Through Mood, Memory and Madira

A Gentle Nudge before You Pour

This isn't your typical cocktail book.

There's no rigid grid of 'vodka-based' or 'rum-forward'. No chapters on 'Essential Techniques' or 'Top 10 Garnishes'. Because India doesn't drink that way. And neither does *Madira*.

This book is meant to be explored the way you'd explore India—by **mood**, **memory**, or **moment**.

Each chapter is a room.

Each drink is a story first, and a recipe second.

Every recipe is rooted in something real—be it a ritual, a region, or a quiet rebellion.

So how should you find your way through it?

There's no single path. But here are eight.

1. Rooted and Ritualistic: The Spirits of Tradition

Choose this chapter when you want to slow down and sink in.

This is a reverent journey through India's ancestral spirits—mahua from the heartland, toddy from the coasts, Arrack from ancient courts. These aren't inventions; they're **resurrections**.

Each cocktail is a **map**—leading to tribal harvests, smoky taverns, and rituals older than the bottle itself.

Read when: You seek grounding, nostalgia, or a drink that feels like a whispered blessing.

2. Bright and Festive: The Cocktails of Celebration

Here's where the party lives.

From Holi's riot of colours to Diwali's soft gold, from sangeets to midnight rooftop laughter—these cocktails are made to raise a glass, and raise your spirit.

Tamarind sours. Mango-mint punches. Rose-saffron spritzes. They don't just toast the moment—they **become** the moment.

Read when: You are hosting, celebrating, or simply in need of a little sparkle.

3. Spiced and Stirred: The Cocktails of Boldness

In India, spice isn't just flavour—it's **philosophy**.

These drinks come in like a whisper and leave like a monsoon.

Masala martinis. Betel leaf bourbon. Ghee-washed rum.

This is where flavour gets **fearless**.

Read when: You are feeling brave, fiery, or ready to shake the status quo.

4. Earthy and Mindful: The Cocktails of Sustainability

This isn't about trend—it's about **truth**.

Inspired by the way our grandmothers cooked: using

everything, wasting nothing. These cocktails turn leftovers into **legends**.

Fermented pineapple smashes. Jackfruit seed Old-Fashioneds. Tamarind peel twists.

Read when: You want something honest, rooted, and deeply Indian. A drink that gives back to the land.

5. Playful and Inventive: The Cocktails of Mischief

This is your wildcard zone.

Where chai mojitos meet *pani puri*, vodka shots, and gulab jamun floats steal the show.

A little nostalgia, a lot of curiosity, and just the right amount of madness.

Read when: You are feeling cheeky, nostalgic, or ready to laugh mid-sip.

6. Quietly Inventive: The Cocktails of Subtle Genius

Not every rebellion needs fireworks.

These drinks are soft-spoken, slow-blooming, and full of **quiet surprises**.

Clove-smoked gin. Curry leaf vermouth. Saffron-washed negronis.

They whisper before they wow.

Read when: You crave elegance, balance, or something that unfolds gently with each sip.

7. Bold and Rebellious: The Cocktails of Creative Anarchy

Here's where tradition gets flipped.

This chapter breaks rules, bends expectations, and dares the palate.

Black garlic sours. Fennel bitters. Wild basil mezcal fusions.

Equal parts **art and anarchy**.

Read when: You want to shock, provoke, or taste something no one's dared pour before.

8. Warm and Soulful: The Cocktails of Comfort

These are your woollen shawls in a glass.

Ginger toddies. Saffron punches. Hot mahua cocoa.

Here, every drink hugs back—with heat, aroma, and depth.

Because sometimes, we don't drink to escape. We drink to **come home**.

Read when: It's cold outside—or inside. When you need warmth, not just in your hands, but in your heart.

Other Ways to Wander

By Story

Let the tale lead you. Sometimes a single line will stay longer than the drink itself.

By Ingredient or Season

Looking for Gondhoraj? Kokum? Jaggery? Flip to the index or the *Seasons of Drinking* guide and sip by the month.

By Region

Each recipe includes its origin. Want to drink the Konkan coast or toast the Khasi Hills? You can travel by taste.

With or Without a Bar Kit

Don't have a jigger? Use a steel *katori*. No shaker? Try a dabba. This book honours **imagination over equipment**.

The Final Stir

This book is more than mixology.

It's mythology—served chilled.

And at the very end of your journey, you'll meet **The Madira Masterpiece**—a drink that distils it all: rooted, festive, bold, mindful, rebellious, and warm.

So pick a chapter. Choose a feeling. And start pouring.

Because when it's done right, a glass doesn't just hold a cocktail.

It holds a **story**.

Mahua Martini

1

MAHUA MARTINI

A Floral, Forest Martini with Kokum

The Story: Two Glasses, One Monsoon

They hadn't spoken much since arriving at the resort tucked between the forests of Pachmarhi, Madhya Pradesh. Anya stared out at the sal trees. Rishi scrolled through his phone. Their anniversary trip was less celebration, more quiet truce.

Then the monsoon came—unexpected and absolute. The sky cracked open, and the two of them darted across the courtyard, taking shelter in the open-sided bar that smelled of woodsmoke and rain-soaked earth.

'You look like you could use something different,' the bartender offered, already reaching for chilled glasses.

Moments later, he placed two golden martinis before them, each crowned with a citrus curl and a single dried mahua flower.

'It's mahua,' he said. 'From the forest here. With a touch of kokum. Locals say it carries memory.'

They sipped.

It was strange and familiar all at once—sweet and earthy, like wildflowers in mist, with kokum's tang weaving through the warmth. Anya closed her eyes as the flavour opened up. Rishi watched her, and something softened.

He smiled faintly. 'You remember Bastar? That little village with the tribal dance?'

She turned to him, surprised.

He grinned. 'The one where you tried to outdrink the old man with the bamboo cup?'

She laughed—really laughed—for the first time in weeks. The kind that made her shoulders drop and her guard fall.

The bartender did not interrupt. He just wiped a glass,

nodded at the rain, and said, 'Mahua's like the monsoon. It doesn't arrive on schedule, but it always knows when it's needed.'

And just like that, the space between them felt a little less distant. One sip became two. Then three.

What Makes This Cocktail Special?

Mahua's Unique Floral Earthiness: A distinctly Indian spirit with a nutty, honeyed profile
Kokum for Bright Balance: A tangy local fruit used in coastal Indian cuisine, now reimagined in mixology
Hyperlocal and Sustainable: Crafted entirely from indigenous, minimal-waste ingredients

Ingredients
(Sourced with Sustainability in Mind)

- Mahua spirit, 60 ml: Floral and forest-fresh
- Kokum reduction, 15 ml: Tangy, deep red, slightly astringent
- Dash of lime zest: For aromatic brightness
- 1 dehydrated mahua flower (garnish)
- Ice cubes: For stirring

How to Make It
(A Ritual of Perfection)

1. Chill a mixing glass with fresh ice.
2. Add 60 ml mahua and 15 ml kokum reduction.
3. Stir gently for 30 seconds.
4. Strain into a chilled martini glass.
5. Add lime zest and float a mahua flower for garnish.

THE FINAL SIP

This mahua martini is more than a drink–it's a conversation between forest, fruit and feeling. It bridges memory and mixology, rain and ritual.

A modern martini. An ancient soul.

2

GONDHORAJ VODKA COLLINS
When Bengal Went Bright and Bubbly

The Story: Letters from Kalimpong

Maya always returned to Kalimpong in the summer. Not for the hill station's postcard beauty, or the wild orchids, or the wool shawls her mother kept sending her back with–but for the letters.

Every summer, there would be one. No name. Just a thin, cream-coloured envelope left at the little café near the monastery gate, addressed to her in soft black ink.

Inside, there would be a story. A memory from a summer past. A riddle. Sometimes, a sketch of the hills. And always–folded neatly into the crease–a sliver of Gondhoraj lime peel, dried and fragrant.

She never asked who sent them. Some loves are better steeped in mystery.

This year, she arrived a day before the monsoon broke. The café's bartender, a young man with a quiet laugh, had something new on the menu. 'Inspired by your envelope,' he said, sliding a tall glass toward her.

It sparkled with soda. A twist of citrus coiled on top.

The scent was unmistakable—Gondhoraj, that bold and haunting lime that Bengal swears by. It rose like memory, like something important just out of reach.

The first sip was all light and brightness—vodka playing backdrop, jaggery syrup curling sweetly around the lime's punch. It fizzed and vanished, like laughter in an old memory.

As she stirred the ice with her straw, the bartender placed an envelope next to her glass. Cream-coloured. Soft black ink.

She did not open it.

Some drinks are like the letters we keep in drawers—not for reading, but for remembering.

What Makes This Cocktail Special?

Gondhoraj Citrus Magic: Bengal's legendary aromatic lime infuses the cocktail with bold, haunting fragrance

Jaggery Syrup Sweetness: Replaces refined sugar with earthy caramel depth

Bright, Clean Base: Vodka allows regional citrus to shine

A Madira Original: A sensory postcard of East India in every sip

Ingredients
(Keeping it Fresh and Sustainable)

- Vodka, 60 ml
- Freshly squeezed Gondhoraj lime, 15-20 ml
- Jaggery syrup (or honey syrup), 15 ml
- Soda water, 120 ml
- Gondhoraj zest (thin strip) for garnish
- Ice cubes—always essential for a true Collins

How to Make It
(A Ritual of Perfection)

1. Fill a tall Collins glass with fresh ice.
2. Add vodka, Gondhoraj lime juice, and jaggery syrup.
3. Stir gently to combine.
4. Top with soda water.
5. Garnish with a long, elegant strip of Gondhoraj zest.

THE FINAL SIP

A drink that whispers summer, nostalgia, and citrus-slick secrets. This isn't just a Vodka Collins—it's a Gondhoraj daydream in a glass.

3

JAGGERY OLD-FASHIONED

A Rustic Reinvention of a Global Classic

The Story: Smoke, Silence, and Second Chances

There was a bar in Jaipur that did not advertise. No neon signs, no Instagram handle—just an old haveli courtyard and a brass lantern by the door. Locals called it *raakh*, meaning ash. Some said it was because of the smoky whiskeys. Others said it was for the stories left behind.

One rainy evening, Arvind walked in—grey at the temples, a slow limp from a life lived hard. He did not come for company, just something warm. The bartender, young but quiet-eyed, slid him a drink without asking.

A short glass. One large cube of ice. The liquid glowed amber. A faint curl of orange peel rested on top, its oils perfuming the air.

'Indian single malt,' the bartender said. 'Sweetened with jaggery syrup. A dash of bitters, a pinch of warmth.'

Arvind sipped. The drink was earthy, not just in flavour, but in feeling. The jaggery hit first—molasses-rich, with a whisper of smoke. Then the spice crept in, cinnamon or maybe star anise, followed by the gentle burn of a highland Indian malt. It was comfort. It was confrontation. It was memory in liquid form.

He did not speak much that night. Just ordered one more.

When he finally left, he nodded once toward the bar. 'Tastes like a fire I did not know I needed,' he said.

And maybe that's the truth of the Jaggery Old-Fashioned. It doesn't fix anything. It just gives you five quiet minutes to feel something real.

What Makes This Cocktail Special?

Indian Single Malt Whiskey: Bold, complex, and locally crafted with Himalayan or Deccan waters

Jaggery Syrup: Made from unrefined cane sugar, offering deep, caramel-like sweetness and Ayurvedic heritage

Indian Aromatic Bitters: Infused with clove, black pepper, and dried orange peel for layered warmth

Optional Warm Spice: A pinch of cinnamon or star anise to round the base notes

Fragrant Garnish: Orange peel or toasted fennel adds a final Indian flourish

Ingredients
(Rooted in Indian Heritage)

- 60 ml Indian single malt whiskey (e.g., Godawan 01, Paul John, etc.)

- 10 ml jaggery syrup
- 2 dashes aromatic bitters (homemade or store-bought, ideally with Indian spice notes: clove, pepper, fennel)
- A pinch of cinnamon or star anise powder
- Large ice cubes—for minimal dilution, maximum elegance
- Dehydrated orange peel or a pinch of toasted fennel seeds

How to Make It
(A Ritual in Stillness)

1. In a mixing glass, combine jaggery syrup, bitters, and spice.
2. Add the Indian single malt and stir gently over ice until chilled.
3. Strain into a short glass over one large ice cube.
4. Garnish with orange peel or lightly toasted fennel seeds.

THE FINAL SIP

This is the Old-Fashioned, reimagined through India's smoky back lanes and sugarcane fields. One sip is heritage. Two is healing.

4

TAMARIND WHISKEY SOUR
A Bold, Tangy Twist on-the Traditional Sour

The Story: Sour Strings and Smokehouse Nights

In the narrow lanes of Lucknow, tucked behind a crumbling haveli and a forgotten music school, there was once a jazz bar called Sour Strings. No signage. Just a sarangi player who played outside on Friday nights and a scent of charcoal from the kebab cart next door.

The regulars came not just for the music or the meat, but for the bartender who spoke little and mixed like a magician. His signature drink? A sour—but not just any. This one had tamarind.

One evening, a young tabla teacher sat at the bar, exhausted after a long rehearsal. He asked for something 'sharp enough to wake the dead but warm enough to remember the living.' The bartender nodded once, reached below, and began to build.

Whiskey—bold and oaky—into the shaker. Tamarind pulp, dark and thick, swirled in. A spoonful of jaggery syrup, two dashes of bitters, and a pinch of toasted *kala namak*, that sulfuric, funky Indian salt that knows how to hum in the background. Shake. Pour. Garnish with a single slice of dehydrated orange.

The first sip? Electric. Tangy tamarind punched through the whiskey's warmth, jaggery rounded the edges, and black salt lingered like a second thought you could not shake.

The tabla player looked up, eyes wide. '*Yeh toh Lucknow ki baarish lagti hai*,' he whispered. (It tastes like rain in Lucknow.)

The bar doesn't exist anymore. But sometimes, when the weather's just right, and you shake the tamarind just so, you can still hear the sarangi playing.

What Makes This Cocktail Special?

Tamarind's Signature Tang: An iconic Indian souring agent gives this drink its bold punch
Jaggery's Molasses Richness: Softens the edges, earthy and full-bodied
Toasted Kala Namak: Adds depth, funk, and unmistakably Indian soul
Indian Single Malt or Bourbon: The bold, warm heart of the cocktail

Ingredients
(Straight from the Indian Kitchen)

- 60 ml whiskey (Indian single malt with a hint of Rajasthan)
- 30 ml tamarind pulp (strained)
- 15 ml jaggery syrup
- 2 dashes aromatic bitters
- A pinch of toasted black salt (kala namak)
- Ice cubes
- Garnish: Dehydrated orange slice or star anise—for aroma and presentation

How to Make It
(A Ritual of Tang and Time)

1. Add all ingredients (except garnish) into a shaker with ice.
2. Shake well for 20 seconds until chilled.
3. Strain into a rocks glass over fresh ice.
4. Garnish: Dehydrated orange slice or float a star anise for aroma.

THE FINAL SIP

A whiskey sour that doesn't whisper—it sings. Tangy, textured, unapologetically Indian. The kind of drink that remembers where it came from.

5

INDIAN SPICED NEGRONI
The Bookshop Edition

The Story: The Bookshop Negroni

The fan clicked in lazy circles overhead, its rhythm as slow as the evening drizzle outside. In the heart of Pondicherry's French Quarter, nestled between a crumbling boulangerie and a banyan-strangled guesthouse, was Sans Serif—a secondhand bookshop that smelled of lemongrass, old paper, and time.

Its owner, Professor Ray, once taught comparative literature at the university. Now, retired and mostly forgotten by his peers, he spent his days arranging books by emotion rather than genre, and his evenings sipping what he called 'a Negroni for those who've loved too much and spoken too little.'

It wasn't a traditional Negroni. Instead of Campari, he used a jamun shrub—tart, earthy, like late-summer regret. He replaced vermouth with a touch of *methi* seed tincture and a drop of paan leaf extract, for bitterness and perfume. His base was always Indian Himalayan gin, wild and piney, just like the Himalayan forests he had never gotten around to visiting.

One monsoon evening, a woman stepped in—grey-haired, graceful. In her hand was a book: *The Essential Rumi*, first edition. Inside the cover was a note in Professor Ray's own handwriting, dated 30 years prior.

'I think this was yours,' she said.

He looked at her, at the book, at the years folded neatly between the pages.

That evening, he made two Negronis. No words were exchanged. Only sips.

The drink was everything it had always been—bitter, balanced, and full of memory.

What Makes This Cocktail Special?

Jamun Shrub Bitterness: A wild, tart fruit reduction that mimics sweet vermouth's depth with an Indian soul

Methi Seed and Paan Leaf Extracts: Aromatic, bitter, and layered like a literary metaphor

Indian Himalayan Gin Base: Infused with juniper and indigenous botanicals

Perfectly Poetic: A sipping drink that pairs with solitude, sonnets, or second chances

Ingredients
(Aromatic and Reflective)

- 30 ml Indian Himalayan gin
- 15-20 ml jamun, shrub
- 5 ml methi seed extract (bitter tincture)
- 2 drops paan leaf extract
- 1 crushed green cardamom pod
- Ice cubes—for slow stirring
- Garnish: Flamed orange peel or dried tulsi leaf

How to Make It
(A Ritual in Balance)

1. In a mixing glass, combine Indian Himalayan gin, jamun shrub, methi extract, and paan leaf drops.
2. Add a crushed cardamom pod if desired.
3. Fill with ice and stir slowly—at least 30 rotations.
4. Strain into a rocks glass over a single large ice cube.
5. Flame an orange peel over the glass or float a tulsi leaf on top.

THE FINAL SIP

Some drinks are not for the party—they're for the pause. This Negroni isn't about forgetting.

It's about remembering...softly.

6

KOKUM AND SPICE VODKA MULE
A Coastal Cooler with a Kick

The Story: Notes from a Thirsty Rickshaw Ride

Goa in May is not very kind. The sun hammers rooftops. Roads shimmer. And the only breeze is the one you chase in a fast-moving rickshaw.

Aarav had just landed after ten years in Berlin. He had come back to open a 'modern Indian cocktail bar'—whatever that meant. But on that first sweltering day, what he really needed wasn't branding advice. It was a drink.

He found it in a small roadside café, the kind with plastic chairs, laminated menus, and a fridge stocked with glass soda bottles. An elderly man in a sleeveless vest was crushing ginger and black pepper with a stone. Next to him simmered a syrup of kokum, jaggery, and cumin.

'Try this,' the man said, pouring the concoction into a battered steel tumbler, topping it with soda and a pinch of kala namak.

Aarav took a sip–and time slowed. The kokum was tart and dark. The ginger soda slapped and soothed. The spices whispered of forgotten kitchens. And the black salt? That was the punctuation mark.

He did not copy the drink. He honoured it.

Back in his bar, the Kokum and Spice Mule became the signature. Served icy cold in hammered copper mugs, garnished with fresh kokum and a curl of ginger.

It wasn't nostalgia. It was now–cool, coastal, and unmistakably Indian.

What Makes This Cocktail Special?

Kokum's Tart Soul: From Konkan to cocktails, this fruit brings depth and a ruby glow
Spiced Ginger Soda: Infused with cumin, coriander, and black pepper for complexity
Jaggery Syrup: Adds earthy sweetness to tame the tang
Kala Namak Magic: A pinch of funk, salt, and soul

Ingredients
(Ice-Cold and Indian at Heart)

- 60 ml vodka
- 30 ml kokum extract or syrup
- 120 ml spiced ginger soda (homemade with ginger, cumin, coriander, and pepper infusion)
- 1 tsp jaggery syrup
- A pinch of black salt (kala namak)
- Fresh kokum slice (for garnish)
- Ice cubes–fill the mug, no skimping

How to Make It
(A Ritual of Refreshment)

1. Fill a copper mug or highball glass with fresh ice.
2. Pour in vodka, kokum extract, and jaggery syrup.
3. Top with spiced ginger soda.
4. Add kala namak and stir gently.
5. Garnish with a fresh kokum slice and optional ginger curl.

THE FINAL SIP

A coastal breeze in a copper mug. Spicy, sour, soulful. This Mule kicks with Indian rhythm and sips like summer.

7

ROSE AND CARDAMOM GIN FIZZ
Where Fragrance Meets Fizz

The Story: The Perfumer's Promise

She always arrived just after sunset.

In the narrow alleys of Lucknow's old city, between perfumeries that hadn't changed in a century, was a little rooftop bar called *Gul*. Named after the Urdu word for 'flower,' it was known only by word of mouth and the scent that drifted from it—rose, cardamom, lime.

The bartender was once a perfumer. He had grown up mixing attars, extracting oils from petals, steeping spices in sandalwood. But when the scent world became too commercial, he walked away—swapping vials for jiggers, distillation for mixology.

Every evening, he made one drink the same way. Rose syrup made from Damask petals. A whisper of cardamom. Fresh lime juice. Botanical gin. Sometimes aquafaba, sometimes not. Always a slow pour of soda to lift the drink into cloud-light elegance.

She came for that drink. Said nothing. Just watched the city breathe beneath them, drank in slow sips, and left without paying.

He never asked why.

Then one day, she did not come. The rose syrup sat untouched. The cardamom stayed sealed. For weeks, he waited.

Until finally, a note arrived—folded into a sachet of dried petals. It simply read: 'I can't come back, but promise me you'll keep making that drink. It reminded me of who I used to be.'

So he did.

And every evening, the bar smelled of memory.

What Makes This Cocktail Special?

Rose Syrup Romance: Organic rose petals deliver delicate sweetness and heady aroma

Cardamom's Whisper: A subtle warmth that lingers on the tongue

Optional Aquafaba or Egg White: Adds creamy texture and cloud-like fizz

Soda Sparkle: Keeps the drink light, refreshing, and balanced

Ingredients
(Aromatic and Naturally Cooling)

- 60 ml floral or botanical-heavy gin
- 30 ml rose syrup (made from organic rose petals)
- 10 ml freshly squeezed lime juice
- A pinch of ground cardamom

- 15 ml aquafaba or egg white
- Soda water—to top up
- Garnish: Edible rose petals and a cardamom pod

How to Make It
(A Ritual in Aroma)

1. In a shaker, combine gin, rose syrup, lime juice, cardamom, and aquafaba/egg white if using.
2. Dry shake (without ice) for 15 seconds to build froth.
3. Add ice and shake again briefly to chill.
4. Strain into a chilled highball or coupe glass.
5. Top with soda water.
6. Garnish with edible rose petals and a cardamom pod.

THE FINAL SIP

This is a drink that doesn't just taste beautiful—it feels like someone remembering your name in a room full of strangers.

8

CINNAMON AND STAR ANISE RUM
A Spiced Delight for Winter Nights

The Story: The Night Watchman's Recipe

Shimla in December slows time.

The tourists are gone, the shops shutter early, and the air smells of pine, charcoal, and forgotten letters. But if you walk uphill past the Ridge and turn at the third lamp post—yes, the one with the cracked base—you'll find a small teahouse that becomes a speakeasy after 10 p.m.

No signboard. Just the clink of firewood and the sound of vinyl jazz.

The man behind the counter is known only as *Baba*. No one knows how old he is, but everyone knows what to order: 'The Watchman.'

He created it, legend says, after falling asleep by a forest fire watch tower in the '70s. He had mixed a flask of rum with cinnamon bark, star anise, and something smoky—maybe salt, maybe memory.

The drink he poured is what he still makes today: dark rum, syrup infused with cinnamon and star anise, a dash of aromatic bitters, and a pinch of smoked Himalayan black salt. Always served over a single ice cube, with a charred cinnamon stick and a star anise pod floating like a compass rose.

It's not sweet. It's not harsh. It's the middle of a sentence you don't want to end.

And if you sit long enough, Baba might tell you what he was watching for, all those winters ago.

What Makes This Cocktail Special?

Dark Rum Base: Full-bodied, smoky, and rich with molasses warmth

Cinnamon and Star Anise Syrup: Infused spice that feels like a fireplace in a glass

Smoked Himalayan Black Salt: Earthy and unexpected, balancing sweetness

Garnishes with Purpose: Charred cinnamon and star anise add both aroma and story

Ingredients
(Warming and Winter-Ready)

- 60 ml dark rum
- 15 ml cinnamon and star anise syrup

- 2 dashes aromatic bitters
- A pinch of smoked Himalayan black salt
- Ice—preferably one large cube to preserve smoothness
- Garnish: Charred cinnamon stick and 1 star anise pod

How to Make It
(A Ritual by Firelight)

1. In a mixing glass, combine rum, syrup, bitters, and black salt.
2. Stir over ice until just chilled.
3. Strain into a rocks glass over one large cube.
4. Garnish with a gently charred cinnamon stick and star anise pod.
5. Sip slowly, preferably near a source of heat and a good story.

THE FINAL SIP

For the nights when the air bites, the stories stretch, and the fire is the only light left.

This isn't just a cocktail. It's a reason to linger.

9

MANGO AND BASIL VODKA SPRITZ
A Bright and Refreshing Tropical Cocktail

The Story: Mango Letters and Basil Days

In a sleepy town just outside Ratnagiri called Pawas, there's a small colonial-era post office that smells faintly of mango wood, ink, and humidity. Every April, it receives a single, handwritten letter addressed to 'The Girl Who Made Mango Ice.'

Thirty years ago, during the summer of '94, a boy named Dev stayed at his grandmother's house in the town. Across the courtyard lived Tara—basil in her hair, mango pulp on her fingers, and always barefoot.

Each afternoon, she would blend mangoes from the orchard with jaggery and lemon juice, drop in a few torn basil leaves, and freeze the mixture into bright orange lollies she handed out to anyone who passed by—postmen, cows, cousins, ghosts of old relatives.

Dev called her his 'summer spritz.'

They lost touch, as kids do. He moved. She stayed. But every year since, he's sent a letter during mango season. No return address. Just a recipe inside—updated, refined, grown-up.

This year's version is what she would've made, if she had a bar instead of a veranda: vodka, Alphonso mango puree, lime, jaggery or honey, fresh basil, and a fizzy splash of soda. Bright, herbal, golden—like a memory that never quite left.

What Makes This Cocktail Special?

Alphonso Mango Purée: India's sunshine in a glass, rich and creamy
Fresh Basil: Adds a green, herbal lift that balances the fruit
Honey or Jaggery Syrup: Natural sweetness with a touch of rustic charm
Soda or Prosecco: Makes the drink light, fizzy, and utterly refreshing

Ingredients
(A Perfect Blend of Sweet and Herbal)

- 45 ml vodka
- 60 ml Alphonso mango purée—ripe and golden
- 15 ml lime juice
- 10 ml honey or jaggery syrup
- A handful of fresh basil leaves
- 60 ml soda water
- Ice cube—always serve it chilled
- Garnish: Basil sprig and mango slice—elegant and aromatic

How to Make It
(A Ritual of Golden Simplicity)

1. In a shaker, muddle basil leaves gently with mango purée and lime juice.
2. Add vodka and honey/jaggery syrup, shake lightly with ice.
3. Strain into a tall glass filled with ice.
4. Top with soda water or Prosecco.
5. Garnish with a fresh basil sprig and mango slice.

THE FINAL SIP

Not every love story ends in letters.

Some end in cocktails—golden, fizzy, and full of basil.

10

SAFFRON AND ALMOND WHISKEY PUNCH
A Decadent Farewell in Gold

The Story: The Cook's Last Shift

The palace had long since faded.

The paint peeled in soft curls. The chandeliers hung lower than they once did. The marble was now more moss than stone. But Juna Mahal had found a second life—as a boutique hotel with yoga retreats, brass bathtubs, and curated 'royal experiences.'

Only one thing remained untouched: the kitchen. And in it, Bade Miyan—the last cook from the royal household, now in his seventies—still arrived each evening to prepare one final course: a cocktail he had once made only for the Nawab himself.

He called it Shahi Pyaala—'The Royal Cup.'

It wasn't showy. But it felt like silk. Into a tumbler went Indian single malt, followed by a touch of almond syrup, saffron threads soaked till golden, and a pinch of cardamom. He added just enough jaggery syrup to echo old desserts, a whisper of pink salt, and stirred it once, like a farewell.

On his last night before retirement, the new hotel chef asked if they could modernize it—maybe add foam or dry ice. Bade Miyan smiled, handed him the glass, and said:

'You don't perfume a memory with smoke.'

They drank on the palace steps. Above them, the sky turned saffron. The glass was empty before the stars came out.

What Makes This Cocktail Special?

Saffron-Soaked Elegance: Subtle, floral, golden
Almond Orgeat Depth: Nutty, sweet, but never overpowering
Jaggery Syrup Complexity: Dark, mineral, molasses-rich
Cardamom and Salt: Balances and lifts the drink with quiet drama

Ingredients
(Refined and Regal)

- 60 ml Indian single malt whiskey
- 15 ml almond syrup (orgeat)
- 1 tsp jaggery syrup
- 4-5 saffron strands—soaked in warm water for 5 minutes
- 1 small pinch of ground cardamom
- 1 small pinch of Himalayan pink salt
- Ice—one large cube preferred
- Garnish: Single saffron thread and toasted almond slice

How to Make It
(A Ritual of Restraint)

1. In a mixing glass, combine whiskey, almond syrup, jaggery syrup, and saffron water.
2. Add cardamom and pink salt.
3. Stir gently over ice.
4. Strain into a rocks glass over one large cube.
5. Garnish with a toasted almond slice and a saffron strand.

THE FINAL SIP

Some legacies are passed in palaces.
Others are stirred in quiet glasses.
This one tastes like both.

11

THE NO-ICE GOA COOLER
Made with Coconut Water and Natural Chill

The Story: The Bartender's Big Problem at a Goa Shack

It was one of those unforgiving April afternoons in Anjuna—the kind where the sand burns your soles and even the breeze feels toasted. The shack was full, the waves were loud, and the tourists were cranky.

Behind the bar stood Ravi Bhau, the man known locally as 'The Mixologist of Mandrem.' His coconut mojitos were legend. His sunrise feni sours? Pure poetry. But just as a fresh wave of sunburnt Brits rolled in, parched and expectant...

The power went out.

No blender. No fans. And worse—no ice. The freezer had turned into a slush swamp.

Groans. Eye-rolls. A couple of Instagrammers already tapping out negative reviews.

But Ravi did not flinch. He cracked open a tender coconut straight from the palm out back. The water inside was already chilled, kissed by the shade and the sea breeze.

He grabbed a bottle of local cashew feni, squeezed in lime, tossed in a few mint leaves, a pinch of sea salt, and gave it all a good shake in an empty coconut shell. No fancy glass. No garnish grid. Just liquid refreshment, Goan style.

He passed the first glass across the counter to a tourist muttering about his 'hydration crisis.'

One sip in, the man leaned back, blinked at the sun, and said, 'Mate...I think I just drank the beach.'

The No-Ice Goa Cooler

And that was that. The No-Ice Goa Cooler became the shack's signature. Served chilled, not frozen. Wild, not watered down. And best enjoyed with bare feet in the sand.

What Makes This Cocktail Special?

No Ice Required: Coconut water stays cool naturally
Local, Sustainable Ingredients: Straight from the palms and the coast
Cashew Feni Kick: Distinctive, tropical, and unmistakably Goan
Herbal and Salty Contrast: Balanced, refreshing, and electrolyte-smart

Ingredients
(Straight from the Tropics)

- 60 ml cashew feni (or white rum as an alternative)
- 120 ml fresh tender coconut water (pre-chilled)
- 10 ml fresh lime juice
- A pinch of Goan sea salt
- 4-5 fresh mint or basil leaves
- Garnish: Strips of coconut flesh and a sprig of basil

How to Make It
(A Ritual of Coastal Cool)

1. In a chilled glass or coconut shell, add lime juice, salt, and herbs.
2. Pour in cashew feni and stir gently.
3. Add chilled coconut water–no ice necessary.
4. Stir again and garnish with coconut strips and basil.
5. Serve barefoot, preferably within earshot of waves.

THE FINAL SIP

No power. No problem. No ice. No regrets.

This is Goa—where even a heatwave tastes like a holiday.

12

THE MUMBAI MASALA HIGHBALL
A Kick of Black Salt and Lemon Zest

The Story: Masala, Midnight, and Marine Drive

It was just past midnight near Marine Drive.

The waves were louder than the taxis. The breeze was thick with humidity, grilled corn smoke, and the dreams of 20 million people.

At a divey rooftop bar above an old Irani café, Nilesh, a self-taught bartender and part-time theatre actor, was hosting his signature 'Masala Mondays.' The usual crowd had gathered—copywriters, stand-up comics, sound engineers, and one guy who swore he used to be in a Coke Studio episode.

Someone asked for 'something that hits like a slap but smiles after.'

So Nilesh did what Mumbai does best—improvised.

He grabbed a bottle of Indian whiskey, added fresh lime juice, a spoon of Jungle honey, and a pinch of kala namak—because if it doesn't smell a little funky, is it even Mumbai?

Then came a dash of roasted cumin, a slice of green chilli, and a generous pour of club soda.

He torched a lime wheel on the side, garnished the drink, and served it with a grin.

The first sip? A riot of salt, heat, fizz, and depth.

Someone muttered, 'This tastes like the best fight I've ever had.'

And so, the Mumbai Masala Highball was born. Bold, chaotic, unforgettable–just like the city that made it.

What Makes This Cocktail Special?

Indian Whiskey Backbone: Rich, oaky, and a perfect match for spice
Kala Namak and Cumin Duo: Funky, earthy, and totally Bombay
Green Chilli Heat: Not overwhelming, just lingering
Masala Soda Vibe: Spicy, fizzy, refreshing, and full of life

Ingredients
(A Cocktail with True Mumbai Swagger)

- 60 ml Indian whiskey
- 10 ml fresh lime juice
- 1 tsp jungle honey
- A pinch of black salt (kala namak)
- A dash of roasted cumin powder
- 1 small green chilli (thinly sliced)
- 120 ml club soda (or masala soda)
- Ice cubes–fill the highball
- Garnish: Charred lime wheel and chilli slice–for drama

How to Make It
(A Ritual in Rush Hour Rhythm)

1. In a tall glass, mix lime juice, jaggery syrup, kala namak, cumin, and green chilli.
2. Add whiskey and fill with ice.
3. Top with club soda or masala soda.
4. Stir once or twice, gently.
5. Garnish with a charred lime wheel and a chilli ring.

THE FINAL SIP

This isn't just a cocktail.

It's Mumbai–poured, spiced, and fizzed.

And trust us, it never asks for permission.

13

COCONUT WATER SPRITZ

Light, Hydrating, and Naturally Delicious

The Story: Spritz at Sunset on the Sandbar

It wasn't on any map.

A tiny sliver of sand that only surfaced during low tide, halfway between Alibaug and nothingness. Locals called it *Chhoti Dharti*–'little earth'. And once a month, for just two hours, it became the most exclusive bar in India.

Anika, a marine-biologist-turned-pop-up-mixologist, had stumbled on the spot during a dolphin survey. She came back with a cooler, a speaker, and a vision: spritzes, sunsets, and serenity.

The drink she served was deceptively simple. White rum or vodka, tender coconut water, a splash of lime, a trace of pink salt (only if the coconut water was extra sweet), and a final fizz of soda water. No syrups. No bitters. Just hydration dressed up for a party.

The first time she poured it, the sky was the colour of roasted cashew skin, and her only customers were two surfers and a turtle.

Now? There's a waitlist.

Everyone wants the Coconut Water Spritz. It's the kind

of drink you sip barefoot, where the dress code is 'salt on skin' and the bill is paid in smiles.

What Makes This Cocktail Special?

Tender Coconut Water: Naturally hydrating, with subtle tropical sweetness
White Rum or Vodka Base: Light and clean, never overpowering
Pink Salt and Lime: Optional trace for balance if needed
Soda Sparkle: Elevates refreshment with a splash of elegance

Ingredients
(A Coastal Minimalist's Dream)

- 45 ml white rum or vodka
- 90 ml fresh tender coconut water–pre-chilled
- 10 ml fresh lime juice
- A trace of Himalayan pink salt
- 90 ml soda water or sparkling coconut water
- Ice cubes (optional, if pre-chilled)
- Garnish: Thin coconut slice and fresh mint sprig

How to Make It
(A Ritual in Refreshment)

1. In a tall glass, add lime juice, base spirit, and optional salt.
2. Fill with pre-chilled coconut water.
3. Add soda water and stir gently.
4. Garnish with coconut slice and mint sprig.
5. Serve cold, with toes in the sand if possible.

THE FINAL SIP

No mixers. No theatrics.
Just liquid calm, kissed by the coast.

14

LEMON LEAF GIMLET

A Garden-to-Glass Classic

The Story: The Tree Outside the Kitchen Window

Every summer, the house smelled like pickles and books.

The old lemon tree outside the kitchen window bore fruit thrice a year, but the leaves? They were evergreen—soft, fragrant, glossy. Dadi would pluck them by the dozen, dropping them into boiling *kadha*, herbal oil, even wedding rice.

But one person saw something different in those leaves.

Sana, her granddaughter—freshly back from a bartending course in Delhi—had returned to visit, lugging a suitcase of spirits and ideas. One lazy afternoon, watching Dadi dry lemon peels on an old steel tray, she noticed the leaves fluttering nearby.

'What do they taste like?' she asked.

'Smell first,' Dadi said.

The scent was unmistakable—lemony, green, a little floral.

That evening, Sana steeped those leaves in Indian gin, mixed it with a little lime peel syrup she had made from pickle scraps, and added just a drop of citrus bitters.

She served it cold, no garnish, no ice—just a chilled glass, clean and green.

Dadi took a sip, raised an eyebrow, and said, 'This is how the lemon tree dreams at night.'

And so, the Lemon Leaf Gimlet was born—fresh, fragrant, and full of quiet wisdom.

What Makes This Cocktail Special?

Lemon Leaf Infusion: Adds citrus aroma without waste
Peel Syrup or Citrus Scrap Cordial: Reduces fruit waste, maximizes flavour
No Ice Shaking: Pre-chill everything to save water
Clean, Crisp Serve: Just glass, just green

Ingredients
(Bright, Lean, and Leafy)

- 60 ml Indian gin
- 20 ml lemon leaf-infused water or gin (infused for 24 hours in fridge)
- 15 ml lime peel syrup or cordial
- 1 dash citrus bitters
- Garnish: None—or a single lemon leaf, if you must

How to Make It
(A Ritual in Restraint)

1. Pre-infuse gin with lemon leaves (overnight in the fridge or for 24 hours).
2. Chill all ingredients before assembling.
3. In a shaker, combine infused gin, peel syrup, and bitters.
4. Shake hard without ice or stir cold if using infused water instead of full gin.
5. Strain into a chilled coupe or stem glass.
6. Serve without garnish—or a single fresh lemon leaf for scent.

THE FINAL SIP

Not all cocktails need a crowd.

Some just need a lemon tree, a quiet kitchen, and one memory made fresh.

15

PINEAPPLE PEEL PUNCH
A Tropical Low-Waste Wonder

The Story: The Ferment on the Fridge Shelf

The fridge was humming like an old harmonium.

Inside it, tucked in a recycled jam jar, was pineapple skin, jaggery, a clove or two, and a vague sense of rebellion. This was Kabir's secret project. Not the bartender Kabir who worked at the rooftop speakeasy in Bandra—but the homegrown, ex-chef, fermentation-obsessed Kabir who believed no fruit should die in vain.

The idea had started when he watched a prep cook toss a mountain of pineapple peels after carving slices for garnishes. It felt wrong—like throwing away sunlight.

So he took them home, added a bit of jaggery, water, and time. Three days later, the jar fizzed back at him—alive, fragrant, tangy-sweet. Pineapple peel punch. Fermented, natural, low-alcohol, and perfect for a new kind of cocktail.

He strained it, added a dash of spiced rum, some lime, and topped it with soda. The result was golden, gently fizzy, complex, and completely unexpected.

He served it the next night at the bar. When asked what it was called, he grinned:

'Waste not, punch later.'

And so, the Pineapple Peel Punch became a quiet legend—sweet with purpose, tart with cleverness, and fizzing with intent.

What Makes This Cocktail Special?

Fermented Pineapple Peel Base: Tangy, natural, and zero-waste
Jaggery Sweetness: Earthy and perfect for fermentation
Spiced Rum or White Rum Flexibility: Adds depth or keeps it fresh
Soda for Lift: Keeps the drink light and bubbly
Eco-conscious and Bar-smart: Uses kitchen scrap, not imported syrups

Ingredients
(Waste-Savvy and Wildly Refreshing)

- 60 ml fermented pineapple peel punch base (see prep below)
- 30 ml spiced rum
- 10 ml fresh lime juice
- 90 ml soda water or sparkling water
- Ice cubes—for service
- Garnish: Pineapple core sliver or spent lime wedge

How to Make the Pineapple Peel Base

1. Save the peels from 1 whole pineapple (wash thoroughly).
2. Add to a jar with:
    - 1.5 cups water + 2 tbsp jaggery or sugar
    - 1 clove or small cinnamon stick (optional)
3. Cover with muslin or loose lid and ferment at room temp for 48-72 hours.
4. Strain and refrigerate. Use within 4 days.

How to Make the Cocktail

1. In a tall glass, combine pineapple peel base, rum, and lime juice.
2. Fill with ice, top with soda, and stir gently.
3. Garnish with a wedge of lime or a pineapple stick.
4. Serve immediately—ideally outdoors.

THE FINAL SIP

From peel to punch, this isn't a drink.

It's proof that flavour has no waste, and creativity has no ceiling.

16

THE NAGPUR NAG
A Bold Whiskey and Orange Concoction

The Story: The Widow and the Snake

They say there's a woman who walks the Nagpur orchards at dusk, dressed in saffron silk, with a sprig of chilli tucked behind her ear.

No one knows her name. Some call her *Naagin Bai*. Others just call her 'the Widow.' Her husband—once a spice trader, now a ghost—left her the orchard and a cellar full of Indian malt he used to sip, neat, with a piece of jaggery.

On winter evenings, when the citrus trees perfume the wind, she sets out a small table under her favourite tree—a crooked old orange tree known to bear fruit laced with fire. Locals whisper that it once grew where a cobra had made its last stand. The fruit's bitterness is said to bite you back.

One night, a young traveller lost his way through the orchards, lured by light, music, and the smell of something smoky and sweet. She offered him a drink–golden, glowing, with a charred orange wheel and a floating chilli. He hesitated.

'Afraid of a little fire?' she asked, her voice like honey with a crackle.

He took a sip.

It hit like citrus lightning–Nagpur orange juice, warm Indian whiskey, a jaggery backbone, a whisper of Bhut Jolokia, and a strange, wonderful finish of smoked black salt.

He blinked. 'What's it called?'

She smiled. 'It doesn't have a name. But it remembers you.'

What Makes This Cocktail Special?

Nagpur Orange Juice: Bright, seasonal, unmistakably Indian
Bhut Jolokia Heat: Adds subtle fire without overwhelming
Jaggery Syrup Depth: For caramel richness
Smoked Black Salt: Adds earth, umami, and mystery
Indian Single Malt Whiskey: Strong enough to balance the boldness

Ingredients
(Fiery and Citrusy)

- 60 ml Indian single malt whiskey
- 30 ml fresh Nagpur orange juice
- 10 ml jaggery syrup
- 1 small slice of Bhut Jolokia chilli (or 2 dried chilli flakes)
- 2 dashes orange bitters
- A pinch of smoked Himalayan black salt
- Ice–large block preferred
- Garnish: Charred orange wheel and whole dried chilli

How to Make It
(A Ritual in Citrus and Smoke)

1. In a mixing glass, add orange juice, jaggery syrup, and bitters.
2. Muddle gently with chilli—do not over-infuse.
3. Add whiskey and smoked salt.
4. Stir over ice to chill and dilute slightly.
5. Strain into a rocks glass with one large ice block.
6. Garnish with a charred orange wheel and whole chilli.

THE FINAL SIP

This isn't for the faint of heart.

It's for those who know that sweetness is always better with a little bite.

17

THE TEKANPUR FIELD POUR
Sugarcane and Mahua Meet Military Grit

The Story: The Cadet's Recipe

Cadet Naveen Kumar wasn't the top marksman at the BSF academy in Tekanpur. He wasn't the fastest runner either. But come survival training week, he had something no one else did—memory and instinct.

Born in a village not far from the forest belt of Madhya Pradesh, he grew up around mahua trees, their flowers gathered by his grandmother each morning in a faded cloth sack. His summers were scented with ferment and sugarcane—a local fusion of fire and nectar.

The red earth of Tekanpur might have hardened his stance and sharpened his salute, but it hadn't dulled his palate.

One evening, during a bushcraft drill, Naveen was tasked with building shelter and prepping a meal under moonlight. He chopped firewood, fashioned a tarp from a poncho, and prepped for the ration pack stew like every other cadet.

Apart from the tasks assigned, he also built a drink—his own small act of flavour and memory, tucked between drills and dusk.

He pulled out a flask of local mahua, mixed it with fresh sugarcane juice he had traded from a roadside cart that morning, added a squeeze of lime, and crushed in a few black pepper seeds and wild curry leaves growing near the base of a neem tree.

No shakers. No glassware. He stirred it with a clean tent peg and poured it into his metal army mug, letting the wild scent rise with the breeze.

When his instructor passed by and curiously raised a brow, Naveen offered a sip.

The officer took it, sipped, and paused—surprised.

'This tastes like protocol-breaking,' he said with a smirk.

Naveen simply shrugged. 'No sir, this is ancestral protocol. Just repurposed for the field.'

What Makes This Cocktail Special?

Fresh Sugarcane Juice: Naturally sweet and refreshing
Mahua: Ancestral, fermented forest spirit
Lime and Wild Herbs: Adds zest and foraged fragrance
Minimalist Prep: A nod to survivalist skill and simplicity

Ingredients
(Rugged, Earthy, and Real)

- 60 ml mahua spirit
- 60 ml fresh sugarcane juice
- 10 ml fresh lime juice
- A few fresh curry leaves (lightly crushed)
- A pinch of freshly cracked black pepper
- Ice cubes (optional, if not on field)
- Garnish: Wild herb sprig or curry leaf

How to Make It
(A Field-Ready Ritual)

1. In a metal mug or glass, mix mahua, sugarcane juice, and lime juice.
2. Lightly crush curry leaves and add to the drink.
3. Sprinkle cracked black pepper.
4. Stir using a spoon (or a clean field-safe tool).
5. Serve with or without ice, garnished with a curry leaf.

THE FINAL SIP

A sip of this is like field training for the soul—raw, rooted, and ready.

18

KASHMIRI KAHWA WHISKEY
Infused with Saffron, Almonds, and Green Tea

The Story: The Hiker and the Hidden Stove

On the third day of the solo trek, the wind turned cruel.

Radha had trained for this hike—across a lesser-known Himalayan pass, surrounded by snow bridges and fir forests—but nothing prepared her for the storm that rolled in from the east. Temperatures dropped. Visibility fell. Her limbs ached, and her flask ran dry.

By dusk, she stumbled onto a stone shelter—roofless but wind-blocked. Inside, tucked under a stack of firewood, she found a miracle: a small copper kettle, a packet of green tea leaves, a jar of jaggery, saffron strands, a few crushed almonds, and—almost absurdly—a bottle of Indian single malt sealed with wax and a tag that simply read:

'For those who make it this far.'

Hands trembling more from awe than cold, she started a fire.

She brewed the tea as instinctively as memory, adding cinnamon, saffron, almonds. Then, a generous pour of whiskey. She did not sip—she closed her eyes and exhaled into it.

It was sweet, spiced, and smoky—like the earth had decided to forgive her for showing up unprepared.

The next morning, the storm was gone. The trail reopened. But Radha left something behind: a note, taped to the kettle—

'The best warmth is the one you find when no one else is looking. Pass it on.'

What Makes This Cocktail Special?

Fresh Kashmiri Kahwa: Fragrant, green, layered with spice
Indian Single Malt: Rich, warming, with smoky undertones
Saffron and Almonds: Luxury and texture in every sip
Optional Bitters: Adds a whisper of citrus complexity

Ingredients
(Aromatic, Spiced, and Cozy)

- 60 ml Indian single malt whiskey
- 120 ml freshly brewed Kashmiri Kahwa (green tea, cinnamon, saffron, crushed almonds)
- 10 ml honey or jaggery syrup
- 1 small cinnamon stick
- 2-3 strands of saffron
- 1-2 crushed almonds or almond slivers
- A dash of orange bitters (optional)
- Garnish: Toasted almonds and cinnamon stick

How to Make It
(A Ritual of Warmth and Memory)

1. Brew a fresh pot of Kashmiri Kahwa (or green tea with saffron, cinnamon, and almonds).
2. While still warm, pour 120 ml into a heat-safe glass or mug.
3. Add whiskey and honey/jaggery syrup.
4. Drop in saffron strands and stir with cinnamon stick.
5. Add a dash of bitters (optional).
6. Garnish with toasted almond slivers and serve immediately.

THE FINAL SIP

This isn't just a winter warmer.

It's a whisper from the valley—steeped in history, poured with quiet fire.

19

THE COORG CAMPFIRE COCKTAIL
Coffee and Whiskey Meet the Wilderness

The Story: Embers and Estate Coffee

The night air in Coorg is thick with mist and memory.

At the edge of a pepper plantation, a group of friends had gathered around a glowing campfire. No resorts. No WiFi. Just silence, forest, and the soft crackle of wood. The forest smelled of wet bark, roasted spices, and leaf mulch. You could hear the pepper vines whisper when the wind passed.

Among the group was Veer, who had once traded his family's 90-year-old coffee estate for a speakeasy in Pune—sharp lights, jazzy signage, the works. But something about serving espresso martinis with bottled syrup had always felt...hollow.

This trip wasn't just a getaway. It was a quiet homecoming.

The others brought marshmallows and packets of chips. Veer brought what mattered: a flask of Indian single malt, a jar of strong estate-brewed coffee, and a tin of thick, caramel-toned date syrup (natural sweetener)—a sweetener his grandmother once used in everything from porridge to pickles.

As the fire burned low to embers, he heated the coffee in a kettle balanced on stones. He poured in the whiskey, stirred in the date syrup, and split a cinnamon stick, searing one end in the fire till it smoked.

He stirred slowly, letting the smoke curl into the mug. The air now smelled like roasted fruit, burnt bark, and winter.

They passed the mugs around. Steam curled into the mountain air. Veer handed one to Raka—his childhood friend who now taught permaculture in Goa. Raka sipped once, then looked at him, surprised.

'This doesn't taste like the city,' he said, 'or even like nostalgia.'

Veer smiled. 'It tastes like I stayed.'

What Makes This Cocktail Special?

Strong Coorg Coffee: Bold, roasted, estate-grown richness
Indian Single Malt: Brings depth and structure
Date Syrup (Natural Sweetener): Adds dark, molasses-like warmth
Charred Cinnamon: Infuses with smoke and spice
Campfire Aroma: Infused with memory, not just smoke

Ingredients
(Smoky, Bold, and Warming)

- 60 ml Indian single malt whiskey
- 30 ml freshly brewed strong Coorg coffee
- 15 ml date syrup + 1 small cinnamon stick (charred)
- 1 dash orange bitters
- Garnish: Coffee beans and a charred cinnamon stick
- Serve hot or warm in a heat-safe mug

How to Make It
(A Ritual of Firelight and Flavour)

1. Brew strong Coorg coffee and keep warm.
2. In a small saucepan or kettle, gently heat whiskey, coffee, and date syrup.
3. Stir with a slightly charred cinnamon stick.
4. Pour into a heat-safe mug.
5. Add bitters (optional).
6. Garnish with a cinnamon stick and coffee beans.
7. Sip slow, ideally next to fire or stars.

Every sip is smoke, spice, and story—as if the forest itself brewed your drink while you weren't looking.

The Kerala Toddy Cooler

20

THE KERALA TODDY COOLER

A Fermented Tropical Delight with a Citrus Twist

The Story: The Boatman's Secret

They say the best drink in Kerala isn't served in bars—it's passed from hand to hand on boats.

Joseph, a backwater boatman, wasn't just known for navigating the narrowest canals. He was known for something else—a small clay bottle he carried tucked into his satchel. Tourists thought it was water. Locals knew better.

It was fresh toddy, tapped that morning from the coconut trees behind his home—gently fermented, slightly fizzy, and brimming with local pride.

One scorching afternoon, a couple from Mumbai boarded his canoe. They were tired, sunburnt, and curious. Joseph, sensing the moment, pulled out his bottle and poured a splash into steel tumblers. But this time, he had a twist.

He added a bit of fresh coconut water, a squeeze of lime, a spoonful of sweetener syrup (natural sweetener), and a pinch of crushed black pepper and toasted cumin. He crushed a few fresh curry leaves between his palms—'for smell,' he said—and stirred it all together.

The drink sparkled with earth, leaf, and sunlight. The couple took a sip—and laughed. It tasted like summer vacation and temple bells.

When they asked for the name, Joseph just smiled:

'It's not a cocktail. It's how we say hello in these parts.'

What Makes This Cocktail Special?

Fresh Toddy Base: Naturally fermented, tropical, and lightly fizzy

Coconut Water and Lime: Hydrating and bright
Crushed Spices and Curry Leaves: Adds complexity and Kerala soul
Natural Sweetener: Balances the citrus and spice

Ingredients
(Tropical, Spiced, and Refreshing)

- 90 ml fresh Kerala toddy
- 30 ml fresh coconut water
- 15 ml sweetener syrup
- 10 ml fresh lime juice
- A pinch of crushed black pepper and toasted cumin
- A few fresh curry leaves
- Ice cubes
- Garnish: Coconut slice and a sprig of curry leaves

How to Make It
(A Ritual from the Backwaters)

1. In a shaker or large tumbler, add toddy, coconut water, lime juice, and sweetener.
2. Add crushed pepper, cumin, and curry leaves.
3. Shake gently or stir, keeping it rustic.
4. Pour into a chilled glass with or without ice.
5. Garnish with a coconut slice and curry sprig.
6. Sip slow, under a banana leaf roof if possible.

THE FINAL SIP

It's more than a cooler.

It's Kerala in a glass—fermented, fragrant, and full of easy joy.

21

THE BANGALORE HIGHBALL

Coconut Water, Gin, and a Dash of Spice

The Story: The Botanist on the Balcony

In Bangalore, the evenings are a thing of art.

Not loud. Not showy. Just slow clouds, a purple sky, and the gentle sound of garden sprinklers ticking under gulmohar trees. On one such evening, in a quiet corner of Indiranagar, a woman named Soumya sat on her balcony, sipping something clear and shimmering.

Soumya wasn't a mixologist. She was a botanist. A quiet observer of plant rhythms—someone who could identify mint from memory and knew which hour tulsi smelled its sweetest.

That day had been long. Labs, lectures, and relentless notifications. She needed a pause—but not the heavy kind. Something hydrating, light, and alive.

She opened her fridge and reached for chilled coconut water, freshly bottled from a vendor she trusted near Ulsoor Lake. Then, a bottle of Indian botanical gin—delicate, floral, and citrusy. She poured equal parts, added a squeeze of lime, and crushed a few fresh curry leaves between her palms. The oils released like memory—bright, green, and unmistakably southern.

Just as she leaned back, her friend from Delhi video-called.

'What's that? A G&T?'

Soumya smiled.

'Nope. It's a Bangalore Highball. You would not get it unless you've smelled rain on red soil.'

What Makes This Cocktail Special?

Fresh Coconut Water: Naturally hydrating with a soft body
Botanical Indian Gin: Delicate, floral, and contemporary
Curry Leaves: South Indian aroma and herbal depth
No Salt or Cumin: Clean, fresh, and breezy

Ingredients
(Garden-Fresh, Light, and Modern)

- 45 ml Indian botanical gin
- 90 ml fresh coconut water (chilled)
- 10 ml fresh lime juice
- 4-5 fresh curry leaves
- Optional: 1 green cardamom pod
- Garnish: Lime peel or a small curry leaf sprig
- Ice cubes (optional)

How to Make It

(As Easy as Evening Breeze)

1. In a highball glass, combine gin, coconut water, and lime juice.
2. Add lightly crushed curry leaves (and cardamom pod if using).
3. Stir gently to blend and infuse.
4. Add ice cubes if desired.
5. Garnish with a lime peel or small curry leaf sprig.
6. Sip slow while watching the light change.

THE FINAL SIP

Clean, calm, and citrusy—the Bangalore Highball is for those who like their cocktail cool and clever, without shouting for attention.

22

CHENNAI FILTER KAAPI OLD-FASHIONED

South Indian Coffee and Whiskey in Bold Fusion

The Story: Brass Tumblers and Broken Rules

In a tiny Mylapore apartment, where jasmine hung from every window and MS Subbulakshmi hummed softly from an old radio, Arvind was doing something slightly sacrilegious.

He was tampering with filter kaapi.

His grandmother would've clicked her tongue, called it a disgrace to the brass *dabara* set. But Arvind—fresh out of a Michelin internship in Singapore—wasn't here to follow rules. He was here to bend nostalgia into new glassware.

That evening, he brewed his filter *kaapi* the old way: dark roast, slow drip, thick as molasses. But instead of adding milk or sugar, he reached for his flask of Indian single malt, a drop of palm jaggery syrup, and two dashes of bitters.

He poured the hot decoction into a chilled glass, added whiskey, stirred slowly, and garnished it with a tiny twist of orange peel and a cracked cardamom pod.

The drink was smoky, earthy, slightly sweet—with a hum of bitterness and memory.

When his friend took a sip, she paused.

'This tastes like...a filter kaapi that grew up and moved abroad.'

Arvind smiled.

'No. It's one that came back home with swagger.'

What Makes This Cocktail Special?

Authentic Filter Kaapi Decoction: Slow-drip, dark, intense
Indian Single Malt: Warm, oaky, adds depth

Palm Jaggery Syrup: Regional sweetness with molasses notes
Bitters and Cardamom: Elegant finish with old-world spice

Ingredients
(Robust, Aromatic, and Bold)

- 45 ml Indian single malt whiskey
- 30 ml strong South Indian filter coffee decoction (cooled)
- 10 ml palm jaggery syrup
- 2 dashes aromatic bitters
- 1 cracked green cardamom pod (optional)
- Garnish: Orange peel twist or roasted coffee bean
- Ice (large cube preferred)

How to Make It
(A Stir of Boldness and Brass)

1. Brew strong filter coffee and let it cool.
2. In a mixing glass, add whiskey, decoction, jaggery syrup, bitters, and cardamom.
3. Stir gently with a large ice cube until well chilled.
4. Strain into a rocks glass with fresh ice.
5. Garnish with orange peel or a coffee bean.
6. Sip with pride, and a nod to heritage.

THE FINAL SIP

It's filter kaapi.
It's old-fashioned.
It's Chennai—if it wore a tux and still rocked Kolhapuris.

23

DARJEELING TEA WHISKEY SOUR
Smoky Whiskey Meets Floral Darjeeling Tea

The Story: A Note from the Hills

Every winter, Megha returned to her grandfather's bungalow in Darjeeling—a two-story home with green shutters, crooked floorboards, and a porch that looked out at the sleeping face of Kanchenjunga.

She came back less for the view, more for the quiet.

He had been gone five years now. But his presence lingered—in the smell of old cedar trunks, the faint sound of sitar music from a forgotten cassette, and the ritual of evening tea he never missed, rain or shine.

He wasn't just a tea planter. He was a storyteller, a whiskey sipper, a letter writer. He measured tea leaves by memory, not scale, and believed a good drink had to taste like both fire and forgiveness.

One evening, tucked inside a yellowing field journal, Megha found a line in his unmistakable scrawl:

'Tea. Whiskey. Lemon. A dash of honey. Shake like the mountain winds. Sip like you are listening to someone long gone.'

She followed it like a map.

She brewed a pot of first flush Darjeeling, cooled it, and added a pour of his favourite Indian single malt. A spoon of forest honey. A squeeze of lemon. She shook it gently and poured it into his old crystal tumbler—the one with the chipped rim.

She sat on his old porch chair, glass in hand, the hills slowly swallowing the light.

It tasted of smoke and flowers.

Of silence and saying goodbye again.

What Makes This Cocktail Special?

Darjeeling First Flush Tea: Light, floral, high-altitude elegance
Smoky Indian Whiskey: Bold and grounding
Honey and Lemon: Classic sour notes with Himalayan soul
Balanced and Bright: Deep yet delicate

Ingredients
(Floral, Earthy, and Balanced)

- 45 ml Indian single malt whiskey
- 30 ml cooled Darjeeling tea
- 15 ml fresh lemon juice
- 10 ml forest honey syrup
- Ice cubes
- Garnish: Lemon wheel and tea leaf sprig or dried tea leaf edge

How to Make It
(A Shake of the Hills)

1. Brew Darjeeling tea strong and let it cool.
2. In a shaker, combine whiskey, tea, lemon juice, and honey syrup.
3. Add ice and shake well until chilled.
4. Strain into a rocks glass or coupe.
5. Garnish with a thin lemon wheel and tea sprig.
6. Sip slowly and picture the hills in winter light.

THE FINAL SIP

Where whiskey meets tea, the past meets pause—and it lingers, long after the glass is empty.

24

THE KHANDWA KISHORE
A Betel Leaf-Infused Highball in Tribute to a Legend

The Story: The Kishore in the Glass

In Khandwa, the sun falls gently—even the shadows feel like they've heard music before.

Every year on August 4th, the town hums a little louder. Old transistor radios come alive. Speakers under paan shops blare 'Khaike Paan Banaraswala'. The municipal garden puts up faded banners with a sketch of Kishore Kumar's wide-eyed smile.

It's not a celebration.

It's a remembering.

That year, Jay came back to Khandwa after twenty years. A sound engineer now living in Mumbai, he had walked through thousands of studios—but none of them echoed like his childhood home, where Kishore's voice was part of every Sunday morning and every heartbreak that followed.

On the evening of Kishore Da's birth anniversary, he found himself alone in his grandfather's courtyard, surrounded by bougainvillea and cassette tapes.

He reached for a bottle of vodka and a paan box left on the wooden ledge—a gift from his grandmother, still filled with betel leaves, gulkand, and fennel seeds. On instinct, he infused the vodka with paan, added a touch of lime, a spoon of rose-fennel syrup, and topped it with soda.

He stirred it slowly. The drink wasn't planned.

It just...happened. Like a tune you hum without realizing.

As he took the first sip, 'Aanewala Pal' played on a neighbour's old radio.

The Khandwa Kishore

He did not toast. He did not smile.

He just closed his eyes and let it flood back—his grandfather's hand on his shoulder, the sound of Kishore laughing between takes, and the sharp sweetness of *meetha* paan handed to him after every family dinner.

The drink was floral. Bitter. Warm. Familiar.

It tasted like Khandwa.

It tasted like coming home.

What Makes This Cocktail Special?

Betel Leaf-Infused Vodka: Herbal, cool, and distinctly Indian
Rose and Fennel Syrup: Inspired by meetha paan
Lime and Soda: Brings brightness and balance
A Tribute in Every Sip: Layered like Kishore Da's voice

Ingredients
(Floral, Nostalgic, and Refreshing)

- 45 ml vodka infused with betel leaves
- 10 ml rose and fennel syrup
- 10 ml fresh lime juice
- 90 ml soda water
- Ice cubes
- Garnish: Fresh betel leaf curl or rose petal

How to Make It
(A Sip in C Major)

1. Infuse vodka with fresh betel leaves for 24 hours, strain before use.
2. In a highball glass, combine infused vodka, syrup, and lime juice.
3. Add ice and top with soda water.
4. Stir gently.
5. Garnish with a curled betel leaf or rose petal.
6. Serve chilled, and let it sing its quiet tribute.

THE FINAL SIP

Not just a cocktail—this is a Kishore Kumar melody in liquid form.

Playful, poetic, and forever unforgettable.

25

THE RAJASTHAN SANDSTORM

Smoked Whiskey with Dry Desert Spices

The Story: The Desert Doesn't Forget

In the quiet stone alleys of Alwar, where the Aravalli winds speak in whispers and old palaces still wear the scent of rebellion, there stands a forgotten hunting lodge turned artist's retreat. Not listed on any map—just known through stories passed between musicians, chefs, and poets.

That evening, Arya—a chef from Delhi—arrived just before sunset. She wasn't there to cook or impress. Just to be still, to taste the land.

Inside the courtyard, as the wind kicked up, the sky turned gold with dust. Arya found shelter under an old archway and sat down beside a small fire pit the caretaker had lit for warmth.

He offered her a brass cup, a wedge of lime, and a simple blend of toasted cumin and dry ginger he used in chai.

She smiled—this was enough.

From her bag, she pulled out a flask of smoky Rajasthan single malt she had picked up in Jaipur. She poured a measure, added a spoon of jaggery syrup, a squeeze of lime, and just a pinch of the spice blend.

No shakers. No garnish.

Just her, the wind, and a drink that tasted like it belonged here.

It was bold, earthy, and comforting—like the desert, once it accepts you.

She took out her notebook and wrote just one line:

'The desert doesn't forget. It just stores everything in silence.'

What Makes This Cocktail Special?

Smoked Indian Single Malt: Deep, earthy, and regionally inspired

Desert Spice Blend: Dry ginger, toasted cumin for a warming kick

Lime and Jaggery: Adds brightness and sweetness without complexity

Minimalist, Bold: Made for firelit evenings and golden skies

Ingredients
(Smoky, Warming, and Minimal)

- 60 ml Indian artisanal single malt whiskey
- 10 ml jaggery syrup
- 10 ml fresh lime juice
- A pinch of toasted cumin and dry ginger blend
- Ice (optional)
- Garnish: None needed—rustic as it is

How to Make It
(Desert-Simple)

1. In a glass or brass cup, add whiskey, lime juice, and jaggery syrup.
2. Add a pinch of the dry spice blend (toasted cumin and dry ginger).

3. Stir gently to blend.
4. Serve with or without ice, depending on mood.
5. Sip beside a fire, and let the silence do the rest.

THE FINAL SIP

This isn't a cocktail for noise.

It's a drink for stillness—for remembering things the wind once told you.

26

HOLI THANDAI MARTINI

A Boozy Take on the Festival Favourite

The Story: Rang, Reminiscence, and a Martini

For Diya, Holi in Indore had always started at 7 a.m. with a steel thali of colours, loud cousins banging dholaks, and her grandmother insisting everyone sip a glass of cold, creamy thandai before the first handful of *gulaal* was thrown.

But it wasn't just Holi that held her heart.

It was Rangpanchmi—five days later—when the city of Indore truly lost its inhibitions.

Every year, Diya and her gang would wake early, pile onto a scooty, and join the legendary Gair—a wild, swirling street parade of colours, drums, DJ trucks, and joyful chaos. Streets packed from Rajwada to Chhatribagh. Water cannons, foam sprays, herbal gulaal, and a million strangers laughing like old friends.

One year, after the madness, drenched and dizzy with colour, she stumbled into a tiny café tucked behind a flower stall. The bartender, grinning and just as colour-soaked, handed her a glass.

'It's thandai,' he said, 'but shaken, not stirred.'

She laughed, took a sip, and paused.

Vodka. Saffron. Almonds. Rose. Ice-cold. Uplifting. Familiar, but new.

That drink tasted like childhood and chaos.

Like tradition with swagger.

Like Indore itself.

She never asked for the recipe. She did not need to.

Holi Thandai Martini

Because now, every year when Rangpanchmi arrives and the playlist gets louder, Diya makes herself that Holi Thandai Martini—clinks it to the past, and sips with a smile still a little stained in pink.

What Makes This Cocktail Special?

Thandai Meets Vodka: A fusion of tradition and modern elegance
Saffron, Fennel, and Almonds: A rich, spiced, and floral experience
A Creamy Martini that's Festive yet Sophisticated: Perfect for Holi or any celebration

Ingredients
(Spiced, Nutty, and Smooth)

- 60 ml vodka (or white rum for a sweeter touch)
- 90 ml fresh thandai
- 10-15 ml saffron syrup
- A dash of rose water
- Ice cubes
- Garnish: Crushed pistachios and edible rose petals—a festive finishing touch

How to Make It
(Festival in a Glass)

1. In a shaker, combine vodka, thandai, saffron syrup, and rose water.
2. Add ice cubes and shake vigorously until chilled and creamy.
3. Strain into a chilled martini glass.
4. Garnish with crushed pistachios and edible rose petals.
5. Serve immediately and let the celebration begin.

THE FINAL SIP

The Holi Thandai Martini is a celebration in every sense—flavours that linger, memories that sparkle, and a spirit that matches the colours in the air.

27

DIWALI SPICED TODDY
A Warming Cocktail Infused with Saffron and Cloves

The Story: Brass Cups and Childhood Bets

Every Diwali, Vineet came home to Pune from wherever life had taken him—Mumbai, London, Singapore. It did not matter. Because home was Diwali night in his parents' courtyard, where uncles argued over *teen patti*, aunties traded *besan ladoos* across the veranda, and the air always smelled like fried snacks and sandalwood incense.

But more than the sweets or the sparklers, what Vineet waited for most was the drink his grandfather always made.

It wasn't fancy. It did not come from a cocktail book.

Just warm fresh *neera*, cloves, cardamom, saffron, and a hint of jaggery. Stirred over the stove, poured into brass tumblers, and passed around with a quiet warning:

'Slow sips. This one's memory-rich.'

That Diwali, Vineet's grandfather was no longer there.

So Vineet stepped into the kitchen.

He added a cinnamon stick to the old toddy base, squeezed in a bit of lime for brightness, and served it in the same brass cups.

No one said much.

But when the drink reached his grandmother's hands, she smiled softly and said:

'Tastes just like him—warm, and impossible to forget.'

Diwali Spiced Toddy

What Makes This Cocktail Special?

Fresh Neera: A nod to toddy traditions with local freshness
Saffron, Clove, and Cardamom: Classic Diwali spices that warm and comfort
Brass Cup Nostalgia: Served the way memories were meant to be sipped

Ingredients
(Spiced, Comforting, and Festive)

- 90 ml fresh neera
- 45 ml dark rum or Indian brandy
- 10 ml jaggery syrup
- 2 cloves + 1 cardamom pod + 1 small cinnamon stick
- 3-4 saffron strands, infused in warm water
- A dash of lime juice–for brightness
- Garnish: Toasted saffron strand or a clove in the cup

How to Make It
(Warm and Stirred)

1. In a small saucepan, gently heat the neera with cloves, cardamom, cinnamon, and jaggery syrup.
2. Let it steep (do not boil) for 5-6 minutes.
3. Add the saffron infusion and stir gently.
4. Remove from heat, strain into a brass or ceramic cup.
5. Add lime juice and optional rum or brandy.
6. Serve warm, not hot–like good conversation.

THE FINAL SIP

A Diwali drink for when the lights dim, the cards are done, and the stories start flowing. Warm, layered, and full of echoes–just like family.

28

MANGO AND MINT SUMMER COOLER
A Refreshing Seasonal Delight

The Story: Mangoes, Mischief, and a Sip of Summer

In Meerut, summer did not start with a calendar. It began when the first Langda *aam* hit the sabzi mandi—tart, green-skinned, and fragrant enough to make the whole street smell like mango pulp and heat.

For Nidhi, childhood was a blur of sunburns, street cricket, and stolen mangoes. Her cousin brothers would climb the trees in their neighbourhood, chuck down the Langdas, and race back before anyone spotted them. Her job? Hide the loot in a metal bucket and sneak in pudina leaves from Dadi's kitchen garden.

They'd mash the mangoes by hand, add mint, a pinch of black salt, and stir it with their fingers until it turned golden and frothy. No blenders. No rules. Just sweet, gritty joy in steel glasses that clinked with laughter.

Years later, in a Delhi café, Nidhi recreated the memory with a twist: Langda pulp, muddled mint, lime, and soda, served over ice with a fancy straw.

She called it a Mango and Mint Summer Cooler.

But every time she made one, she had grin and say:

'Iss mein dhoop bhi hai, daant bhi, aur Dadi ke ghuye hue aam bhi.'

What Makes This Cocktail Special?

Langda Mango Pulp: Regional, nostalgic, tangy-sweet perfection

Mint and Lime: Bright and refreshing

No Added Sugar Needed: The mango does all the talking
Optional Black Salt: A wink of North Indian summer soul

Ingredients
(Tangy, Fresh, and Hydrating)

- 60 ml vodka or white rum
- 90 ml fresh Langda mango pulp (strained)
- 5 ml jaggery syrup (optional, only if mango is under-ripe)
- 5-6 mint leaves, muddled
- 10 ml fresh lime juice
- A small pinch of black salt (optional)
- 90 ml soda water
- Ice cubes
- Garnish: Mint sprig and a mango slice

How to Make It
(Chill, Stir, Sip)

1. In a shaker, gently muddle mint leaves with lime juice.
2. Add mango pulp and vodka (if using); include jaggery syrup only if needed.
3. Add ice, shake gently, and strain into a tall glass over fresh ice.
4. Top with soda water and stir lightly.
5. Garnish with a mint sprig and mango slice.
6. Serve chilled—and lean back like it's a summer in UP.

THE FINAL SIP

Sweet without trying. Cool without ice cubes.
This is mango-season nostalgia, bottled.

29

THE BOLLYWOOD NIGHTCAP
Masala Chai Meets Feni in a Bold Night Drink

The Story: The Bollywood Nightcap

On the final day of her first film shoot, Zoya did not stay for the wrap cake. She stayed behind—watching as the gaffer rolled up cables, the set dimmed down to shadows, and someone quietly turned off the fog machine.

Versova at 3 a.m. wasn't loud anymore. It hummed softly, like the backbeat of a lullaby you could not name.

She walked back to her tiny rented flat, shoes in hand, clothes scented with sweat, chai, and ambition. Her roommate, half-asleep and always dramatic, handed her a steaming mug.

'It's *feni* masala chai. You've earned it.'

Zoya raised an eyebrow. 'You put Goan feni in my chai?'

'Call it a nightcap. Call it a plot twist.'

She sipped it—clove, cardamom, jaggery, the fire of feni beneath the comfort of tea—and leaned back into the bean bag, letting her muscles finally unclench.

A moment passed.

Then her phone buzzed: A message from the director. One line.

'You were incredible. I hope you are ready for what's next.'

She grinned.

There were no violins. No slow-motion turn. Just Zoya in an old T-shirt, sipping spiked chai, knowing that the credits hadn't rolled yet.

This wasn't the end.

This was her interval.

What Makes This Cocktail Special?

Goan Cashew Feni: Smoky, earthy, a bold replacement for whiskey
Spiced Masala Chai Base: Comforting and rich
Jaggery and Cardamom: A naturally sweet, warming blend
Perfect for Late Nights: Especially after wrap-ups, heartbreaks, or brilliant scenes

Ingredients
(Bold, Spiced, and Soothing)

- 60 ml Goan cashew feni
- 90 ml fresh masala chai
- 10 ml jaggery syrup
- 1-2 saffron strands
- A dash of nutmeg
- Garnish: A clove-studded orange peel or a cinnamon stick

How to Make It
(Warm and Bold)

1. Brew fresh masala chai with black tea, cardamom, clove, and a hint of cinnamon.
2. Strain and pour into a small saucepan on low heat.
3. Add jaggery syrup, saffron strands (if using), and stir.
4. Turn off the heat and add feni.
5. Pour into a warm ceramic or glass cup.
6. Garnish with clove-studded peel or cinnamon stick.
7. Sip slowly, while the world winds down.

THE FINAL SIP

This isn't your usual chai.

It's the director's cut—spiked, smouldering, and still rolling.

30

THE VILLAGE FEAST RESCUE
Palm Toddy Blended with Fresh Sugarcane Juice

The Story: The Day the Toddy Ran Dry

In a small village just outside Thanjavur, where the breeze smells of wet earth and jasmine, the annual temple feast was more than a meal—it was a ritual. A moment when families returned, neighbours gathered, and time slowed just enough for stories to taste sweeter than dessert.

Gopal had been in charge of the toddy for ten years. A retired schoolteacher with a silver beard and a habit of humming old film songs, he took pride in one thing—his toddy never ran out.

Until that year.

The festival crowd was bigger. The summer, hotter.

And by mid-afternoon, as drums echoed from the temple gate, the last drops of toddy were being scraped from the bottom of the pot.

There was silence. Then whispers. Then rising panic.

Because in the village, not serving toddy at a feast was like forgetting to light the lamp before a prayer.

Gopal said nothing. He simply walked to the small clay pot he had kept in his kitchen—a reserved batch. Saved quietly. Out of habit. Out of respect.

He poured the toddy into the large vessel. Then crossed the dusty road to the sugarcane press near the old well. The boy there—once his student—filled two brass vessels with cold, green sugarcane juice, handing them over like a family heirloom.

Back at the feast, Gopal stirred the cane juice into the

toddy, added a pinch of crushed fennel, a squeeze of lime, and said nothing.

One sip. Then two. Then smiles.

It was light, sweet, and oddly comforting—like home, rediscovered.

Later, someone asked him what the drink was called.

Gopal looked out at the banyan tree full of laughing children, the elders leaning back with steel tumblers, and simply said:

'A rescue. With a secret only the toddy knows.'

What Makes This Cocktail Special?

Fresh Palm Toddy: Earthy, fermented, deeply local
Sugarcane Juice: Crisp, clean, and sweet without heaviness
Fennel and Lime: Adds coolness and lift to balance the blend
Non-alcoholic or Lightly Spiked: Naturally fermented, depending on the toddy used

Ingredients
(Rustic, Sweet, and Seasonal)

- 90 ml fresh palm toddy
- 90 ml fresh sugarcane juice + 1 tsp lime juice—for brightness
- A pinch of crushed fennel seeds
- Ice (optional, or serve slightly chilled)
- Garnish: A tender vetiver root sprig or a fresh lime wheel

How to Make It
(Rural, Refined, Real)

1. In a clay or steel vessel, combine toddy and sugarcane juice.
2. Stir in lime juice and fennel.

3. Pour into a steel or ceramic tumbler.
4. Serve chilled, but not over-iced—let the natural flavours shine.
5. Sip slowly, preferably under a tree or beside a memory.

THE FINAL SIP

A drink that reminds you of resourcefulness, rhythm, and how sometimes the best recipes are born from nothing but heart and a little bit of reserve.

31

GOAN CASHEW FENI NEGRONI
A Twist on the Classic with Local Cashew Liquor

The Story: Bitter, Bold, and Beautiful

Rohan was never one for sweet drinks. Or sweet endings.

A Goan by birth but Mumbaikar by ambition, he had spent years fitting into suits, elevator pitches, and glass-clink Friday nights. His go-to was always the Negroni—strong, serious, never sugar-coated. Just like him.

But on a slow evening back home in Saligao, sitting on his grandmother's *balcao* surrounded by plumeria blooms and monsoon nostalgia, something shifted.

His uncle, a quiet man with a louder palate, placed a drink in front of him:

'Your Negroni. But grown here.'

It was feni, not gin.

Jamun shrub instead of Campari.

A dash of kokum reduction instead of vermouth.

Rohan took one sip and blinked.

It was bitter, bold, and wildly unfamiliar—yet somehow intimate. Like flipping through your childhood diary and seeing your own handwriting, but in another language.

He did not say a word.

Just looked out at the coconut trees swaying like old uncles and thought:

'Maybe roots don't ground you. Maybe they remind you who you used to be.'

And in that moment—glass in hand, memories stirred, no garnish—Rohan did not feel like he had come home.

He felt like home had found him.

What Makes This Cocktail Special?

Goan Cashew Feni: Funky, earthy, bold
Jamun Shrub: Tart, vibrant, and beautifully bittersweet
Kokum Reduction: Adds complexity, depth, and regional richness
No Fuss, No Frills: Just stirred truth in a lowball glass

Ingredients
(Local, Loud, and Stirred)

- 60 ml Goan cashew feni
- 30 ml jamun shrub
- 30 ml kokum reduction
- Ice cubes—for controlled dilution
- Garnish (optional): A slice of dried jamun or a fresh kokum petal

How to Make It
(Stirred, Not Rushed)

1. Add feni, jamun shrub, and kokum reduction into a mixing glass with ice.
2. Stir gently but firmly for 30 seconds—no shaking, no shortcuts.
3. Strain into a chilled old-fashioned or lowball glass over fresh ice.
4. Garnish lightly or serve bare—it doesn't need dressing.
5. Sip slow, preferably under open sky and old stories.

THE FINAL SIP

Some drinks impress.
Some linger.
This one reminds you where you were before you forgot.

32

CHILLI-TAMARIND MARGARITA

Tequila Meets Indian Street Flavours

The Story: A Twist of Lime and Trouble

It started with a fight.

Not a big one. Just enough eye-rolls and sarcasm to cut the misty tension of a wet summer evening in Shillong.

Nikhil and Rhea, two cocktail pop-up artists and ex-everythings, had landed at the same indie music festival in Ward's Lake gardens. She had a booth slinging street-style tacos with green chilli oil. He was doing northeast spice infusions with tamarind and citrus.

Somewhere between her teasing 'your rim game is weak' and his smirking 'you still can't balance heat,' the sparks became a dare.

That night, Rhea made a drink to shut him up.

She borrowed his *imli* pulp, added her top-shelf tequila, a splash of fresh lime, a kiss of orange liqueur, and just enough jaggery syrup to make it wickedly smooth.

She rimmed the glass with red chilli powder and crushed chaat masala, handed it over, and said:

'Let's see you balance this.'

He took one sip, coughed (dramatically), grinned, and said:

'This is dangerous. Like us.'

By the end of the night, they weren't fighting anymore.

They were tweaking the recipe together, under fairy lights, while a local band played old Bollywood jazz covers in the distance.

And just like that, the Chilli-Tamarind Margarita was born—hot, sharp, slightly sweet, and never boring.

Chilli-Tamarind Margarita

What Makes This Cocktail Special?

Tequila Meets Tamarind Pulp: Bold base, earthy tang
Jaggery Syrup: Adds body and Indian soul
Chilli + Chaat Masala Rim: A full-on flavour explosion
Perfect for Festivals, Flirting, and Fireworks

Ingredients
(Zingy, Bold, and Beautiful)

- 60 ml silver tequila
- 30 ml tamarind pulp
- 15 ml fresh lime juice
- 10 ml jaggery syrup
- 10 ml orange liqueur
- Rim mix: Red chilli powder + crushed chaat masala + sea salt
- Ice cubes
- Garnish: Lime wedge + slit green chilli (optional but dramatic)

How to Make It
(Spiked Street Magic)

1. Rub a lime wedge around your glass rim and dip it into the chilli-chaat-salt mix.
2. In a shaker, combine tequila, tamarind pulp, lime juice, jaggery syrup, and orange liqueur.
3. Add ice and shake hard for 15-20 seconds.
4. Strain into the prepared glass over fresh ice.
5. Garnish with lime wedge and/or slit chilli.
6. Serve immediately with a warning: This one bites back.

THE FINAL SIP

Not your usual margarita.

This one tells stories, flirts with fire, and leaves you craving the sequel.

33

SMOKED CLOVE MANHATTAN

A Deep and Smoky Rendition of the Manhattan

The Story: Notes of Smoke and Memory

Every evening at exactly 7:12 p.m., Mr Menon would light a clove cigarette, pour himself a drink, and step onto the narrow balcony of his Chennai apartment—the one overlooking the old rain tree, where time dripped slowly between leaves.

He had once been many things—a jazz pianist in Colaba, a college professor in Trivandrum, a translator of Neruda into Malayalam. But no one really knew.

What people did know was this: his drinks were poetry in a glass.

Always stirred. Always sharp. Never loud.

One rainy Thursday, his niece Ananya arrived unannounced—heartbroken from a love that had promised permanence, but left quietly, like an actor after the final bow.

She did not speak much. He did not ask.

Instead, he pulled out an old bottle of Indian single malt, a jar of clove syrup he had made the week before 'for the smell of it,' and a single fat clove, which he lit like incense and tucked under an overturned glass to let the smoke settle.

He stirred the drink slowly, poured it gently, and handed it to her with a whisper:

'This is a memory drink. Let it burn a little.'

She took one sip, paused, and whispered,

'This...doesn't fix anything. But it helps.'

He nodded, and with the softest smile said:

'Some things are made to be sipped, not solved.'

What Makes This Cocktail Special?

Indian Single Malt or Rye: Smooth, full-bodied, with depth
Homemade Clove Syrup: Warm spice that lingers long after the sip
Bitters and Smoke: Adds complexity, memory, and mood
Aromatic and Emotional: Perfect for rainy nights, jazz, or silence

Ingredients
(Smoky, Spiced, and Stirred)

- 60 ml Indian single malt whiskey
- 20 ml clove syrup
- 2 dashes aromatic bitters
- 1 fat clove
- Ice cubes
- Garnish: Clove-studded orange peel

How to Make It
(Still, Slow, and Stirred)

1. Use a torch or match to light a clove; trap it inside your glass with a metal coaster or bowl to capture smoke.
2. In a mixing glass, combine whiskey, clove syrup, and bitters over ice.

3. Stir slowly for 30 seconds until cold and silky.
4. Remove the glass dome; let the smoke escape.
5. Strain the drink into the smoked glass.
6. Garnish with clove-studded orange peel or nothing at all—it speaks for itself.

THE FINAL SIP

For nights that deserve music, memories, and just enough burn to remind you it was real.

34

MUMBAI PORTSIDE MARTINI
A Bold Mix of Port Wine, Brandy, and Spices

The Story: Salt in the Air, Spice in the Glass

Colaba. 11:45 p.m.

The rain had finally stopped, leaving the streets slick with nostalgia. Inside an old wood-panelled bar tucked near the docks, Aryan—a writer who hadn't written in months—sat nursing a glass of brandy and regret.

He wasn't looking for inspiration. Just something warm. Something familiar.

The bartender, an old Goan with a faded 'Merchant Navy' tattoo, walked over and asked,

'You ever tasted Bombay's old ports?'

Aryan blinked. 'The wine?'

'No. The city. The spice. The nights where deals were inked over clove-scented glasses.'

And with that, he stirred up a drink.

A dark splash of port wine, a generous pour of Indian brandy, a clove-and-cinnamon tincture, and a dash of sea salt on the rim for bite.

It was smoky. Spiced. Almost...coastal.

Aryan took a sip and felt the city again. Not the real estate and deadlines—the Bombay of whispered alliances, backroom stories, midnight music, and quiet power.

He wrote that night. A lot.

The piece was never published.

But he never forgot that drink.

What Makes This Cocktail Special?

Port Wine and Brandy Fusion: Colonial, coastal, classy
Clove and Cinnamon Tincture: A nod to dockside spice trades
Sea Salt Rim: Salty, bold, and unmistakably Bombay
Dark, Stirred, Seductive: The Martini's brooding cousin

Ingredients
(Spiced, Smoky, and Bold)

- 45 ml Indian brandy
- 30 ml port wine
- 1 tsp clove and cinnamon tincture
- 2 dashes aromatic bitters
- Rim: Coarse sea salt + crushed pink peppercorn (optional but striking)
- Ice cubes
- Garnish: Orange twist or clove-studded lime wheel

How to Make It
(Strong, Still, Story-Rich)

1. Chill your martini glass and gently salt the rim with sea salt and pink pepper mix.

2. In a mixing glass, add brandy, port wine, tincture (or spiced syrup), and bitters.
3. Add ice and stir slowly for 25-30 seconds until chilled but not diluted.
4. Strain into the prepared martini glass.
5. Garnish with an orange twist or clove-studded lime wheel.
6. Sip slow. Preferably after dark. Preferably alone or with someone worth listening to.

THE FINAL SIP

Old ports never close. They just turn into flavours waiting to be poured again.

35

HIMALAYAN JUNIPER GIN SMASH
Wild Juniper and Mountain Honey Cocktail

The Story: Mist, Firewood, and a Smash

In a tiny village near Ziro, tucked deep into Arunachal's evergreen folds, where every morning smells like moss and memory, Tashi ran a bar that wasn't really a bar.

It had no signboard. Just three mismatched stools, a shelf of forest-sourced bottles, and a small clay fireplace that never fully died out. The locals called it 'The Corner', because that's exactly what it was—a corner to warm your fingers, quiet your thoughts, and meet something older than yourself.

Tourists rarely found it. Locals did not need to.

It was a bar for the in-between hours, where conversations moved slow and laughter did not echo too loudly.

One November evening, just as the early dusk hugged the peaks in layers of violet, Ayaan arrived.

A writer from Bengaluru with cracked boots, ink-stained fingers, and a novel he had nearly given up on. His voice was gone. His rhythm, lost somewhere between deadlines and disinterest.

He wandered into The Corner and stood there, unsure. The place wasn't on Google. The air smelled of juniper smoke and wet wood. It did not feel like a bar. It felt like a pause.

Tashi did not ask questions. He never did.

He crushed foraged wild juniper berries, sharp and resinous, added a pour of local Himalayan gin distilled from barley and pine, a spoonful of dark village honey, a few leaves of torn mountain mint, and squeezed in a thumbprint of wild lime. Then he stirred it gently into a frost-kissed steel tumbler and slid it across the counter.

'This one doesn't talk much,' he said. 'But it listens.'

Ayaan took one sip.

It was herbal, cold, and slightly feral at first. Then came the warmth—the sweet, smoky hum of honey, the clean finish of gin, and the grounding calm of mint.

He sat down slowly. The fire crackled. A dog snored somewhere behind the counter. The mist thickened outside the single-glass window.

And for the first time in weeks, the words came back.

Not all at once. Not perfectly.

But enough to fill a page.

What Makes This Cocktail Special?

Wild Juniper and Mountain Honey: Forest-forward and herbal

Himalayan Gin: Clean, bold, and deeply botanical
Foraged Flavours, Honest Technique: Crushed, not fussed
Served Cold but Meant to Warm the Soul

Ingredients
(Forest-Crushed and Crisp)

- 60 ml Himalayan gin
- 1 tsp crushed wild juniper berries
- 15 ml mountain honey syrup
- 10 ml fresh lime juice
- 4-5 fresh mountain mint leaves, hand torn
- Crushed ice
- Garnish: Mint sprig or a thin curl of lime peel

How to Make It
(Crushed, Stirred, and Centering)

1. In a shaker or steel tumbler, muddle the juniper berries and mint leaves gently.
2. Add gin, lime juice, and honey syrup.
3. Fill with crushed ice and shake gently—not too hard.
4. Strain into a steel or clay cup filled with fresh crushed ice.
5. Garnish with a mint sprig or lime curl.
6. Serve cold. Let the silence do the rest.

THE FINAL SIP

A drink for forest paths, quiet minds, and stories that bloom slowly—like the mist.

36

LITCHI AND BASIL SPRITZ

A Fragrant and Refreshing Summer Drink

The Story: A Border, a Breeze, a Basil Leaf

In Phuentsholing—or as old-timers still call it, Fursiling—there's a rhythm that flows smoother than paperwork.

Here, Bhutan and India don't divide—they mingle.

Trucks hum across the line, monks trade glances with schoolkids, and the breeze doesn't bother with nationalities.

Namit, a young civil engineer on a break from Kolkata, had come to visit a cousin posted nearby. But the town held him longer than expected.

On his second day, lost more in thought than in direction, he stumbled upon a garden café with no name—just a bamboo gate, a prayer flag, and the smell of fruit and herbs in the air.

The woman behind the counter, Sonam, was in her forties, barefoot and gentle-eyed. She did not ask what he wanted—she simply noticed the tired slouch in his shoulders.

Without a word, she reached into the backyard, plucked five litchis from a sagging branch, and pinched a handful of wild Bhutanese basil from beside her grandmother's prayer wheel.

Back in the shaded kitchen, she muddled the fruit and herbs, added a pour of clear local grain whiskey, stirred in a spoon of forest honey, squeezed a lime, and topped it with sparkling spring water cooled in a clay jug.

She placed the glass in front of him and said:

'This isn't Bhutan. And it isn't India. This is just here. And it's enough.'

Namit took a sip. It was fragrant, light, and startlingly

real—like a conversation with someone you did not know you missed.

He sat quietly.

And for the first time in months, he did not want to leave, fix, or move.

He just wanted to stay. Right there. In that afternoon. In that drink.

Because some places don't offer epiphanies.

They offer a pause. And in that pause, sometimes, you remember who you were before the world told you who to be.

What Makes This Cocktail Special?

Fresh Litchi and Basil: A floral-fruity-herbal symphony
Clear Local Grain Whiskey: Light, earthy, and distinctly sub-Himalayan
Forest Honey and Lime: Balanced sweetness and citrus edge

Topped with Sparkling Water: Clean, bright, and blissfully simple

Ingredients
(Summer-Born and Border-Free)

- 45 ml clear local grain whiskey (or vodka if unavailable)
- 5-6 fresh litchis, peeled and de-seeded and 5-6 fresh basil leaves
- 10 ml forest honey syrup
- 10 ml fresh lime juice +90 ml sparkling water or soda
- Ice cubes + Garnish: Basil sprig and a litchi half

How to Make It
(Soft, Stirred, and Sincere)

1. In a shaker, muddle the litchis and basil gently.
2. Add whiskey, honey syrup, lime juice, and a few ice cubes.

3. Shake lightly—just enough to chill and mix.
4. Strain into a tall glass filled with fresh ice.
5. Top with sparkling water.
6. Garnish with a basil sprig and half a litchi on the rim.
7. Serve with silence or soft music—this one doesn't shout.

THE FINAL SIP

Not a cocktail. A climate. A feeling. A fragrance.

And the softest way to say—stay.

37

CHIKOO BEACH FIZZ

A Creamy, Spiced, Sunset-in-a-Glass Cocktail

The Story: Bordi, Bright Light, and a Fizz That Remembers

In Bordi, where chikoo trees stretch long like memories and the sea stays too quiet to be called a tourist spot, Ishaan had arrived to forget a birthday.

His own.

He wasn't running away—just stepping aside. The beach was empty. The sky was pink. And the only music came from the rickety speaker behind Meher aunty's beach stall, where the breeze always carried a mix of cinnamon and old Parsi records.

'You don't look like you want a cola,' she said, eyeing him with the kind of affection that makes you feel like a kid, no matter your age.

‘What do you have?’ he asked.

She pointed to a basket of overripe chikoos, their skin wrinkled, their sugar at its peak.

‘Beach fizz,’ she said with a wink. ‘Made it for my daughter’s wedding once. People still ask about it more than the bride.’

She scooped the chikoo flesh into a jar, added a pinch of dry ginger, a squeeze of lime, a glug of white rum, a dash of cinnamon, and shook it over crushed ice. Then came the surprise—a splash of soda water—to cut the cream, to lift the sugar, to bring the fizz.

The first sip was impossible to place. Creamy but sharp. Rich but light.

Like a spiced beach milkshake that grew up, got a passport, and never came back.

Ishaan took another sip and watched the waves lick the rocks.

He did not feel like escaping anymore.

The birthday had arrived. Quietly. Gently. With a fizz.

And somehow, that felt like the best kind of celebration.

What Makes This Cocktail Special?

Fresh Chikoo ulp: Creamy, caramel-like tropical base
White Rum and Dry Ginger: Bright, warm kick
Served over Crushed Ice: Beach bar perfection

Ingredients
(Creamy, Tropical, and Lively)

- 60 ml white rum
- 90 ml ripe chikoo pulp
- 10 ml fresh lime juice + 5 ml jaggery or honey syrup
- A pinch of dry ginger powder and a pinch of ground cinnamon
- 60-90 ml soda water (chilled)

- Crushed ice
- Garnish: Lime wheel + a thin slice of chikoo

How to Make It
(Shaken, Fizzy, and Free)

1. In a shaker, add chikoo pulp, lime juice, rum, dry ginger, cinnamon, and syrup (if needed).
2. Shake over crushed ice till frothy and chilled.
3. Pour into a tall glass over fresh crushed ice.
4. Top with soda water and stir gently.
5. Garnish with a lime wheel and a thin chikoo slice.

THE FINAL SIP

Not every celebration needs a song. Sometimes, a creamy fizz, a quiet beach, and one perfect sip is all it takes to remember you are exactly where you need to be.

38

BANANA AND RUM PUNCH

A Creamy Banana-Infused Tiki-Style Drink

The Story: Silk Routes, Lost Recipes, and Brass-Tumbler Memory

Kishor never meant to come to Burhanpur.

His bags were packed for New York. His visa was stamped. But his mother insisted—'At least visit your mama once before you leave the country. It's been ten years, beta.'

So here he was. Hot train, dusty roads, and a sleepy town he had spent years ignoring.

But Burhanpur has a way of remembering you, even if you forget it.

In the 17th century, this wasn't just a fortress—it was a frontier.

The last Mughal outpost before the Southern wilds.

Banana orchards sprawled across black soil, feeding traders and emperors. Bananas were mashed into toddy, simmered with jaggery and clove, turned into the kind of drinks no history book ever mentioned—just grandmothers and folk songs.

That afternoon, in his mama's crumbling haveli, Kishor found a few soft bananas in a basket by the window.

The same kind his grandfather used to mash with jaggery for energy.

The same kind his grandmother once used in warm, spiced *payasam*.

He felt something shift.

In that quiet kitchen, he mashed the bananas.

Added a pour of dark and white rum, a dash of chilled coconut milk, a bit of lime, and a pinch of his grandmother's old spice mix—nutmeg, cardamom, jaggery.

He stirred it into a brass tumbler, the way they used to stir tea during stories.

The first sip hit slow. Creamy. Grounded. Slightly naughty. Utterly familiar.

His mama passed by and laughed:

'Tastes like something your nani might've made—if she had a bottle of rum.'

Kishor smiled, still looking out at the banana trees bending in the evening light.

'Maybe she left it behind...in the fruit.'

What Makes This Cocktail Special?

Overripe Banana Pulp: The sweet, earthy soul of the drink
Dark and White Rum Blend: Richness with a bright tropical lift
Jaggery and Spice: Ancestral warmth in every sip
Coconut Milk: Smooth, creamy, deeply coastal
Brass Tumbler Optional. Regret Not Drinking It? Unlikely.

Ingredients
(Bold, Creamy, and Spiced)

- 60 ml banana pulp
- 30 ml dark rum + 30 ml white rum
- 45 ml chilled coconut milk
- 10 ml lime juice + 10 ml jaggery syrup
- A pinch of nutmeg and a pinch of cardamom powder
- Ice cubes
- Garnish: Toasted banana chip + a dusting of nutmeg

How to Make It
(Smooth, Spiced, and Slow)

1. In a shaker, add banana pulp, both rums, coconut milk, lime juice, jaggery syrup, and spices.
2. Fill with ice and shake hard until frothy and chilled.
3. Double strain into a chilled tumbler or rocks glass over fresh ice.
4. Garnish with a toasted banana chip and a whisper of nutmeg.
5. Sip slowly—preferably barefoot, somewhere warm.

THE FINAL SIP

A drink that doesn't impress on arrival—it lingers, then speaks.

Like home. Like heritage.

Like the one visit that changed everything.

39

PINEAPPLE AND CURRY LEAF SMASH
A Tropical Delight with a Herbal Touch

The Story: Spice, Memory, and Pineapple Skin

In a sleepy village outside Kumarakom, where canoes glide through coconut canals and the breeze always smells a little like cardamom and salt, Meera was trying to recreate her grandmother's old summer recipe.

It wasn't a dish.

It was a drink.

A strange, golden thing made from pineapple scraps and curry leaves, served from a steel jug that was always colder than expected.

She remembered it vaguely—the way it fizzed slightly on the tongue, the whisper of heat beneath the fruit, the way her grandmother crushed the curry leaves with her palms before dropping them in.

Now, as an experimental bartender visiting from Kochi, Meera stood on the same tiled kitchen floor decades later, holding a ripe pineapple and a branch of freshly picked dark green *kariveppila*.

She chopped, smashed, stirred, and spiked.

She added a splash of dark rum, a dash of jaggery

syrup, fresh pineapple pulp, lime, a pinch of black salt, and crushed curry leaves.

Poured it over ice, strained it into an old brass tumbler, and tasted.

The sip was...time-travel.

Sweet and sharp. Bright and earthy. Then—a soft whisper of salt that pulled everything into place.

Outside, the rain began tapping the tiled roof in sync with her smile.

Inside, the curry leaves still crackled faintly in the leftover pulp.

Sometimes the recipe isn't in the ingredients.

It's in the memory of hands that made it first.

What Makes This Cocktail Special?

Fresh Pineapple Pulp: Sweet, juicy, tropical core
Curry Leaves and Black Salt: Herbal depth with umami sharpness
Jaggery Syrup and Lime: Brightened sweetness
Dark Rum: Adds richness and balance

Ingredients
(Tropical, Herbal, and Well-Rounded)

- 60 ml dark rum
- 60 ml fresh pineapple pulp
- 10 ml fresh lime juice and 15 ml jaggery syrup
- 6-8 fresh curry leaves, lightly crushed
- A pinch of black salt
- Ice cubes
- Garnish: Fried curry leaf or a charred pineapple wedge

How to Make It
(Crushed, Stirred, and Seasoned)

1. Lightly toast or crush curry leaves to release their oils.
2. In a shaker, muddle pineapple pulp and curry leaves.
3. Add lime juice, jaggery syrup, rum, black salt, and ice.
4. Shake hard for 10-15 seconds.
5. Double strain into a chilled brass or glass tumbler over fresh ice.
6. Garnish with a crisp curry leaf or a charred pineapple wedge.
7. Serve with monsoon music or under a fan turning slow.

THE FINAL SIP

A drink that doesn't beg to impress—it lingers, like steam on stone floors, reminding you salt was always the secret.

40

WATERMELON AND BLACK PEPPER COLLINS

A Spiced, Juicy Twist on a Collins

The Story: Chilled Fruit, College Mischief, and Chachaji's New Favourite

It was summer break, and Vedant, a third-year engineering student, had reluctantly landed in Katak to spend a week with his cousins.

The WiFi was spotty. The heat stuck like ghee.

And Chachaji's rules were as rigid as the steel lunchboxes he carried to his shop.

'No cold drinks. No fancy-shmancy fridge cocktails. We drink nimbu-pani here, not nightclub water,' he declared every time he saw Vedant near the freezer.

So, naturally, the experiments began when Chachaji wasn't home.

One afternoon, in the back kitchen, Vedant found a chunk of ice-cold watermelon, some black pepper, a bottle of soda, half a lime, and the last bit of his smuggled vodka mini from hostel.

He mashed the watermelon, cracked in some black peppercorns, added lime, honey, and vodka, shook it all over ice, and topped it with fizz from an old glass soda bottle.

Just as he and his cousin were clinking steel tumblers, Chachaji walked in.

Busted. He sniffed. Squinted. Took the leftover glass.

Tasted it. Paused. Then: 'Hmmm. This is...not bad. This is hydration with ambition.'

By sunset, Chachaji was pouring it for himself in his brass lota.

Vedant grinned and scribbled the recipe on the back of a pharmacy bill.

That summer, the 'Watermelon-Black Pepper Collins' became a Katak classic.

And Chachaji? He just called it 'That good soda thing Vedant made.'

What Makes This Cocktail Special?

Fresh Watermelon Juice: Juicy, cooling, perfectly summery
Cracked Black Pepper: Spicy, unexpected, elevates the fruit
Lime and Honey: Tangy-sweet balance with warmth

Ingredients
(Bright, Bubbly, and Bold)

- 60 ml vodka
- 90 ml fresh watermelon juice + 10 ml fresh lime juice
- 10 ml honey syrup (1:1 honey and warm water)
- 1/4 tsp freshly cracked black pepper
- 90 ml soda water (chilled)
- Ice cubes
- Garnish: Watermelon wedge + a tiny sprinkle of pepper on top

How to Make It
(Quick, Chilled, and Cheeky)

1. In a shaker, add watermelon juice, vodka, lime juice, honey syrup, and black pepper.
2. Fill with ice and shake for 10-15 seconds.
3. Strain into a tall glass filled with fresh ice.
4. Top with chilled soda water.
5. Stir gently, garnish with a watermelon wedge and just a whisper of cracked pepper.
6. Serve immediately—with mischief in your eyes.

THE FINAL SIP

It's summer in a glass. A fridge raid. A rule bent.

And the taste of something you'll make again—whether Chachaji allows it or not.

41

KASHMIRI NOON CHAI WHISKEY

Himalayan Salt, Saffron, and Warm Whiskey

The Story: Salted Tea Meets Whiskey and Local Gossip

Anya wasn't in Kashmir for soul-searching—she was there for flavour-hunting. A food journalist from Bangalore, she was two days into a homestay in Ganderbal, charming her way through *wazwan* kitchens and stirring things she probably shouldn't.

When her host, Aunty Shabeena, served her a proper cup of noon chai—salty, pink, and steaming—Anya sipped politely, smiled faintly...and then did what she always did:

'What if we added whiskey?'

Shabeena nearly dropped the bakarkhani.

'The tea is sacred!' she said.

'Exactly,' Anya grinned. 'Sacred things deserve to get toasted.'

Later that night, when everyone else was tucked under kangris, Anya stayed in the kitchen, fiddling with spices like a DJ with a playlist.

She brewed green tea leaves with a pinch of soda, coaxed it into that perfect salmon hue, added a few strands of saffron, and then—gently—poured in a warm, peaty Indian single malt.

She added just enough Himalayan pink salt, a dash of cream, and whispered an apology to tradition.

The first sip?

Creamy. Salty. Aromatic. Bold.

Like a chai that dared to party.

By morning, even Shabeena was sneaking sips—though she called it 'medicinal.'

Kashmiri Noon Chai Whiskey

Now? Anya's Instagram reel of #NoonChaiWhiskey has over 2M views, and somewhere in Ganderbal, someone's whispering:

'She added what to the chai?'

What Makes This Cocktail Special?

Noon Chai Base: Pink, creamy, and naturally salted
Warm Indian Whiskey: Bold, smoky, adds winter heat
Saffron and Himalayan Salt: Aromatic elegance meets mountain minerals
Creamy Finish: Comforting, but with an edge

Ingredients
(Spiced, Silky, and Rebel-Worthy)

- 3 tsp Kashmiri green tea leaves +1/4 tsp baking soda (to turn it pink)
- 300 ml water
- 60 ml Indian single malt whiskey
- 1/4 tsp Himalayan pink salt + 3-4 strands saffron
- 60 ml full-fat milk or cream and 1 tsp sugar or jaggery syrup
- Garnish: A floating saffron strand or rose petal

How to Make It
(Brewed, Spiked, and Brilliant)

1. In a small saucepan, bring 300 ml of water to a boil.
2. Add green tea leaves and baking soda. Stir and simmer until the water turns a deep reddish pink.
3. Add saffron and salt. Simmer gently for 5-7 minutes.
4. Strain and return to low heat. Stir in milk or cream to get a soft pink colour.
5. Add whiskey and sugar (if using). Stir gently—do not boil.
6. Pour into warm mugs or copper cups.

7. Garnish with a saffron strand, rose petal, or a small dusting of nutmeg.

THE FINAL SIP

It's pink. It's salty. It's spiked. And yes—your nani might judge you.

But she'll probably ask for a sip too.

42

SPICED APPLE TODDY

Warm Apple Cider Infused with Cinnamon and Nutmeg

The Story: Firewood, Spice, and the First Frost

Kiran hadn't planned on staying in Munsyari longer than two nights. The trip was just a pause—a breath between two cities, two jobs, two versions of herself.

But the storm came early that year.

Snow fell like silence, thick and fast, coating rooftops and cutting off roads. The whole village slowed, as if the mountains themselves were telling everyone to wait, to listen, to stay.

Inside the wood-panelled guesthouse, Amit—her childhood friend turned reluctant mountain host—lit a fire and rummaged through a spice tin older than their friendship.

'I'm going to make you something to warm your bones and maybe...melt a few regrets,' he said, half-joking.

He started with a pot of fresh apple juice, cloudy and fragrant from a nearby orchard.

Then, with the precision of someone used to storms, he added a cinnamon stick, a shaving of nutmeg, a few cloves, and a star anise, letting them bloom gently over the flame.

As the scent filled the room, he stirred in a spoon of dark honey, a squeeze of lemon, and finally, a healthy pour of Indian single malt–smooth, smoky, the kind that tells you stories without words.

He ladled it into a mug and passed it to Kiran without a word.

The first sip hit her slowly.

Warmth bloomed in her chest. The sweetness of apple, the comfort of spice, the quiet fire of whiskey.

And something else–a familiar calm she hadn't felt in years.

By the time she reached the bottom of the mug, the snow outside had slowed.

So had her heartbeat.

She looked at Amit, who was pretending not to watch her reaction, and softly said,

'I think I forgot how to feel like this.'

He smiled without looking up.

'That's why you needed to come back.'

What Makes This Cocktail Special?

Fresh Apple Juice: Sweet, tangy, naturally comforting
Cinnamon, Nutmeg, Cloves, Star Anise: Layered winter warmth
Indian Single Malt Whiskey: Adds depth, smoke, and heart
Honey and Lemon: Balanced sweet and bright finish
Slow-simmered and Soul-settling: Just like the best evenings

Ingredients
(Warming, Spiced, and Steeped in Comfort)

- 75 ml fresh apple juice

- 60 ml Indian artisanal single malt whiskey
- 1 cinnamon stick, 1 whole star anise, 2 cloves
- A pinch of freshly grated nutmeg and 10 ml fresh lemon juice
- 1 tbsp dark honey (or jaggery syrup)
- Optional: A tiny slice of fresh ginger (for extra warmth)
- Garnish: Thin apple slice and a cinnamon stick

How to Make It
(Simmered, Stirred, and Soulful)

1. In a saucepan, gently heat apple juice over medium heat.
2. Add cinnamon, star anise, cloves, nutmeg, and optional ginger.
3. Let it simmer for 5-7 minutes, allowing the spices to infuse.
4. Stir in honey and lemon juice.
5. Turn off the heat and add the whiskey—never boil alcohol.
6. Strain into a large mug or heatproof glass.
7. Garnish with a thin apple slice and a cinnamon stick.
8. Serve warm, ideally by firelight or wrapped in a shawl.

THE FINAL SIP

A toddy for winter's first sigh.

A drink that doesn't ask questions—just melts a little of whatever you carried in.

43

HYDERABADI SAFFRON BRANDY FLIP

A Rich, Creamy Mughal Cocktail

The Story: Silk, Saffron, and a Grandmother's Winter Ritual

In the heart of Old Hyderabad, past the lanes of Irani cafés and crumbling pearls of forgotten mansions, Zameer's family had a tradition.

Every winter, without fail, they'd gather in their grandmother's haveli on the first Friday of December. It wasn't tied to a festival or a calendar—it was a ritual she had invented after her wedding, calling it *'Garmiyon ka Vidai'*—a farewell to warmth and a welcome to woollen shawls, *badam halwa*, and late-night games of carrom.

Even after she passed, the tradition remained. And now, Zameer—quiet, culinary, the least likely host—had somehow inherited it.

The lights were strung. The cousins had arrived. And the old haveli buzzed like it remembered what to do.

But Zameer? He had only one job: 'Make the welcome drink.'

He went to the spice chest—still lined with velvet—and took out a tiny glass vial of saffron, wrapped in the corner of his grandmother's old handkerchief.

He cracked an egg yolk, whisked in jaggery syrup, added a pour of Indian brandy, a splash of warm milk, a pinch of cardamom, and just the faintest dash of rose water.

He stirred it slow. Poured it into cut-glass goblets. Floated a saffron strand on top.

The first sip?

Silky. Golden. Rich like a sherwani and just as soft.

Later, as the cousins fought over rummy and chachis

debated recipes, Zameer quietly raised a second glass—this one placed beside a black-and-white photo of his grandmother in her silk shawl.

And whispered, 'You always knew how to warm up a room.'

What Makes This Cocktail Special?

Saffron and Cardamom: Classic Hyderabadi royal flavours
Indian Brandy: Warm, smooth, aromatic base
Egg Yolk and Milk: Rich, velvety texture with deep winter comfort
Rose Water and Jaggery Syrup: Floral, earthy sweetness to round the drink
A Cocktail that Tastes like Silk and Stories

Ingredients
(Golden, Spiced, and Regal)

- 60 ml Indian brandy
- 1 egg yolk
- 20 ml jaggery syrup + 30 ml warm full-fat milk (not boiling)
- 3-4 saffron strands
- A pinch of cardamom powder and A few drops of rose water
- Ice cubes
- Garnish: A saffron strand or pinch of edible silver leaf

How to Make It
(Rich, Ritualistic, and Just Right)

1. In a shaker, combine the egg yolk, jaggery syrup, and cardamom.
2. Add soaked saffron milk, warm milk, rose water, and brandy.

3. Fill with ice, and shake hard for 15-20 seconds until thick and frothy.
4. Double strain into a coupe or cut-glass goblet and garnish with saffron strand or edible silver leaf.

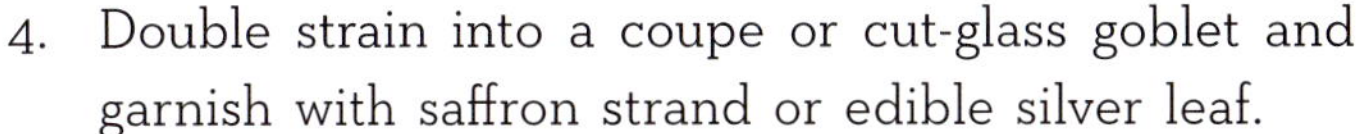

THE FINAL SIP

A drink fit for velvet cushions, old photographs, and quiet evenings that deserve to feel royal. One golden pour at a time.

44

GARAM MASALA HOT TODDY

A Bold Indian Twist on a Winter Classic

The Story: Masala, Moonlight, and a Bonfire That Did Not Forget

Chandigarh winters had their own kind of silence.
Not sad. Just slow.

That week, Ankit was back home, crashing at his mami's place while figuring out if he still wanted to move to Pune. The city was colder than he remembered—not just in weather, but in memory.

One evening, the family decided to light a bonfire in the backyard.

A few chairs, a pile of shawls, and the smell of roasted peanuts in the air. Someone played Jagjit Singh from a phone speaker that refused to stay charged.

Ankit disappeared into the kitchen. Quietly.

He opened nani's old masala box, the one with the

wobbly lid. Still smelled like clove and cinnamon and warm laughter.

In a small pot over the outdoor stove, he boiled water. Added a pinch of garam masala.

A splash of lime. A spoon of jaggery. And then–a generous pour of whiskey.

He stirred it slowly, letting the spices open in the steam.

When he returned to the fire, he passed around brass tumblers of the hot, amber drink–one for each cousin, and one placed quietly beside his grandmother's old garden stool.

The first sip was fire and memory. Sweet, spiced, and just a little defiant.

Chacha took a sip, raised his brow, and said,

'This...is not nani's chai.'

Ankit smiled. 'No. But it remembers her anyway.'

What Makes This Cocktail Special?

Classic Indian Garam Masala: Deep, warming, and nostalgic
Indian Whiskey: Smoky and smooth, perfect for cold nights
Jaggery and Lime: Balanced sweetness and bright citrus lift
Served Hot: Meant for shawls, bonfires, and good stories

Ingredients
(Spiced, Steamy, and Soulful)

- 60 ml Indian whiskey
- 150 ml hot water
- 1/2 tsp garam masala + 10 ml fresh lime juice
- 1 tbsp jaggery syrup (or honey)
- Optional: 1 clove or a small cinnamon stick
- Garnish: Lime wheel + a pinch of garam masala on top

How to Make It
(Steeped, Stirred, and Shared Outdoors)

1. In a small saucepan or kettle, heat the water with garam masala and optional whole spices.
2. Simmer for 3-4 minutes to let the flavours steep.
3. Remove from heat and stir in jaggery syrup and lime juice.
4. Add whiskey and stir gently.
5. Strain into heatproof brass or ceramic tumblers.
6. Garnish with a lime wheel and a faint dusting of garam masala.
7. Serve hot—ideally under stars, beside a fire.

THE FINAL SIP

It's not chai. It's not tradition.

It's memory, spice, and a good idea whispered to the fire.

And it might just warm more than your hands.

45

BLACK TEA AND GINGER WHISKEY SMASH

Where Chai Grows a Backbone

The Story: Lights, Camera, Collapse...and the Comeback in a Cup

2:58 a.m.

On the Mumbai set of *Mumbai Masala*, things were going downhill fast. The crew looked like ghosts. The dancers were sitting cross-legged in costume. And Karan Kapoor, the lead actor, was chewing his dialogue like it was cardboard.

'This chai is doing nothing,' he groaned, tossing his cup onto a prop scooter.

'Sir, we need real energy,' the assistant director mumbled, head buried in a clipboard he hadn't updated in hours.

That's when Babu Bhai, eternally underestimated and always two steps ahead, stepped in.

'You want chai to grow a backbone?' he said, adjusting his cap. 'Hold my flask.'

He grabbed the remaining stash of strong black tea, still simmering.

Sliced up fresh ginger, threw in a pinch of cracked black pepper, smashed cardamom, and sugarcane jaggery syrup—the kind that caramelizes into dreams.

Then came the backbone:

30 ml Indian whiskey + 30 ml Goan cashew feni.

He added a whisper of lime juice, stirred hard, and poured the hot smash into cutting chai glasses that suddenly did not seem so innocent.

Karan took one sip and stood upright.

The spot boys stopped yawning.

And Shankar Sir? He shouted, 'ROLLING!' before anyone could question what was in the cup.

One take. One shot. One perfectly saved scene.

As the sun crept up over the skyline and the wrap party playlist kicked in, the crew knew what they owed their comeback to.

Not caffeine. Not adrenaline.

But a chai that chose chaos—and grew a backbone.

What Makes This Cocktail Special?

Strong Black Tea: Bold, tannic, and grounding
Fresh Ginger + Black pepper: A one-two punch of heat
Indian Whiskey + Cashew feni: Soulful, sharp, and completely awake
Jaggery Syrup: Earthy sweetness to bind it all
Cutting Chai Attitude, Cocktail-level Depth

Ingredients
(Spicy, Smoky, and Smash-Worthy)

- 60 ml strong brewed black tea (use Assam cooled slightly)
- 30 ml Indian whiskey
- 30 ml cashew feni
- 10 ml jaggery syrup
- 10 ml fresh lime juice + 1 tsp grated fresh ginger
- 1 pinch cracked black pepper + 1 crushed cardamom pod
- Ice (for shaking)
- Garnish: Lime wheel + ginger slice or star anise

How to Make It
(Stirred, Smashed, and Served with Swagger)

1. Brew strong black tea and let it cool slightly (not hot, not cold).
2. In a shaker, muddle ginger, cardamom, and jaggery syrup.
3. Add whiskey, feni, tea, lime juice, and cracked pepper.
4. Add ice and shake vigorously for 10-15 seconds.
5. Strain into a steel cutting chai glass or lowball tumbler with fresh ice.
6. Garnish with a lime wheel and a sliver of ginger or star anise.
7. Serve with a side of dramatic dialogue.

THE FINAL SIP

It's chai with a kick, feni with a mission, and the kind of smash that'll keep the cameras rolling long after the scene ends.

46

THE SUNDARBANS JUNGLE PUNCH

Tropical Simplicity with Delta Soul

The Story: Guava, Rum, and the River That Doesn't Apologize

Rupak did not pack for cocktails.

He packed for salt water, camera batteries, and one too many power bars. The Sundarbans wasn't a holiday—it was a living map of mud trails, tiger whispers, and sky that changed its mood every twenty minutes.

He had been tracking footprints since dawn, following a guide with a machete and a boatman who smelled of fish and wisdom.

By late afternoon, the tide had turned, the air was thick with stillness, and the only thing stronger than his sunburn was his thirst.

They pulled the boat over near a small tea hut, more roof than walls, more shadow than shelter.

Khokon da, the boatman, grinned. 'You want Coke? Or Sundarban style?'

Rupak chose right.

Khokon grabbed a steel tumbler, added a few slices of fresh green guava plucked from the tree out back, crushed them with his thumb, poured in a dollop of palm jaggery syrup, a solid splash of dark rum, and finished it with a pinch of black salt and red chilli powder.

He stirred it once. No garnish. No glassware.

Just river, sweat, and story.

Rupak took one sip—and everything slowed down.

It was tart, earthy, hot and sweet—like getting slapped by the jungle, then hugged by it.

The Sundarbans Jungle Punch

They sat there in silence, watching a crocodile slide past like it was late for something important.

And in that moment, under a frayed tarpaulin, with mud on his boots and guava seeds in his teeth, Rupak felt like the Sundarbans had poured him a drink...and told him not to ask for seconds.

What Makes This Cocktail Special

Green Guava: Foraged, fibrous, refreshingly tart
Palm Jaggery Syrup: Sweetness that's rooted in the delta
Indian Dark Rum: Smooth, strong, and honest
Chilli and Black Salt: Punch, heat, and a little wildness

Ingredients
(Rough, Real, and Ready)

- 45 ml Indian dark rum
- 2-3 slices green guava, lightly crushed (seeds and all)
- 15 ml palm jaggery syrup + a pinch of black salt
- A pinch of red chilli powder (or cracked pepper)
- Splash of river-cold water or crushed ice
- Garnish: Guava wedge (optional, or stuck on a twig for style)

How to Make It

1. In a steel tumbler, add the guava and jaggery syrup.
2. Add salt, chilli powder, and pour in the rum.
3. Stir with anything that won't rust.
4. Add a splash of water or ice, if you've got it.
5. Sip slow, don't overthink, and let the jungle finish your sentences.

THE FINAL SIP

You don't find this cocktail on a bar menu.

You find it when you've run out of map, and the river decides you've earned a story.

47

THE MEGHALAYA WILDFLOWER FIZZ

Inspired by Northeast India's Floral Heritage

The Story: A Trail, a Pact, and a Fizz That Bloomed in the Mist

Ira and Neha had one month.

Thirty days between finishing engineering and starting their new jobs in Pune's corporate towers.

And they did not want resorts. They wanted roots.

So they flew to Meghalaya, bought two second-hand trekking poles, packed trail mix they never ate, and set off on the Dympep trail—a winding route known for its orchids, overgrown steps, and clouds that came and went like shy companions.

By the third day, they were drenched, tired, and blissfully phone-free.

Somewhere near a mossy stone bench, they stopped.

Neha pulled out the tiny flask of local rice spirit she had picked up in a market. Ira had stashed wildflower honey and a half-cut citrus fruit from a roadside vendor.

Together, they crushed a few petals they'd been saving, squeezed the citrus, added a spoon of honey, and poured it all into their steel bottle.

Then came the splash of soda water, still cold from the stream they'd dipped it in.

The drink sparkled. The trail paused. And the sky broke open just long enough to show them how high they'd come.

They called it the Wildflower Fizz.

And when they finally descended the mountain, they weren't just graduates anymore.

They were two girls who'd climbed, created, and claimed something of their own.

What Makes This Cocktail Special?

Local Rice Spirit: Smooth, earthy, light-bodied
Wildflower Honey: Floral sweetness with subtle depth
Citrus Juice: Bright, native tang (use Khasi lemon or lime)
Sparkling Water: Effervescent lift to mimic the mist
Wild Petals or Herbs: A fragrant touch of the trail

Ingredients
(Bright, Misty, and Bloom-Worthy)

- 45 ml local rice spirit (or vodka/white rum as an alternative)
- 15 ml wildflower honey syrup
- 15 ml fresh citrus juice
- 90 ml chilled sparkling water
- A few edible wildflower petals or bruised lemongrass leaves
- Ice cubes
- Garnish: Citrus twist and one wildflower petal (if available)

How to Make It
(Trail-Ready and Trail-Tested)

1. In a flask or steel tumbler, mix the rice spirit, citrus juice, and honey syrup.

2. Stir until the honey is well blended.
3. Add chilled sparkling water and stir gently.
4. Drop in a wildflower petal or lemongrass for fragrance (if you found one).
5. Sip slow, while the clouds roll in—or just before they part.

THE FINAL SIP

Light as mist, wild as memory, and just grounded enough to remind you: you did not get here by scrolling. You hiked. And that fizz? It knows.

48

ANDAMAN COCONUT BREEZE

Rum, Tender Coconut, and Pandan Simplicity

The Story: A Hammock, a Heartbeat, and the Salt in the Sip

Rhea hadn't spoken to anyone in two days.

She had left behind an inbox full of things-that-could-wait and booked a one-way ticket to Havelock Island—no plan, no plus one, no deadlines.

Each morning, she walked barefoot across the beach, let the tide kiss her ankles, and listened to the waves say all the things no one else did.

The sun was high on the third afternoon when she found a small thatched beach hut with a handwritten board: *'Juice, Rum, Peace.'*

Inside, the bartender—a quiet man with a salt-bleached ponytail—was grating something green into a shaker.

'What is that?' she asked.

He smiled. 'Screw pine leaf. Locals call it pandan. Smells like vanilla. Grows behind the shack.'

He added fresh tender coconut water, a dash of sea salt, and a healthy pour of dark island rum.

Shook it once, slow and easy.

Poured it over ice in a cut coconut shell.

The aroma hit her first—sweet, grassy, clean.

Then came the sip:

Cool coconut, soft vanilla, rum warmth, a whisper of salt.

It did not taste like a cocktail.

It tasted like a secret the sea had kept just for her.

Rhea stayed another week.

Sometimes she still doesn't know why.

What Makes It Special:

Tender Coconut Water: Hydrating and pure
Local Dark Rum: Rich and mellow
Grated Pandan (Screw Pine) Leaf: Delicate vanilla aroma
Sea Salt: For balance and minerality
Ice and Simplicity: Because the island doesn't rush

Ingredients
(Fresh, Coastal, and Whisper-Light)

- 60 ml Indian dark rum
- 120 ml fresh tender coconut water (chilled)
- 1 small piece of grated pandan leaf
- A pinch of sea salt
- Ice cubes or crushed ice
- Garnish: Coconut shaving or a twist of pandan leaf

How to Make It
(Island-Style Simplicity)

1. In a shaker, combine coconut water, rum, grated pandan, and sea salt.
2. Shake gently with ice until chilled.
3. Strain into a cut coconut shell or chilled lowball glass.
4. Garnish if you like—or sip it bare, the way the island would.

THE FINAL SIP

It smells like shade.

Tastes like a nap after a swim.

And feels like the island saying—'Stay one more day.'

49

MANALI MULLED WINE

Red Wine Infused with Mountain Spices

The Story: A Bad Mood, a Good Fire, and a Drink She Did not Mean to Get Right

Tanu wasn't meant to be there.

Aditya's chalet party in Manali was invite-only. And while they had broken up 'maturely,' the Instagram reel of him stirring wine next to someone new had its own spice.

So, she arrived with two friends and walked straight into the kitchen, where a pot of red wine sat warming—destined to be mediocre and photogenic.

Tanu looked around, half-daring herself, and added whatever she could lay her hands on: Onge peels, cinnamon sticks, cloves, local apple jam, black pepper, just for chaos

She stirred once. No one saw.

Just left it there, like a firework with no fuse.

Later, when the wine ran low and the DJ's speaker died, someone poured the 'spiced batch' into mugs.

A hush fell.

Even Aditya blinked.

'Who made this?' he asked, sipping again.

Tanu, across the room, tasted it for the first time herself.

Warm. Deep. Citrus. Slightly sweet. Comforting, confusing...kind of brilliant.

She raised an eyebrow, then looked down at her mug.

'I wasn't even trying.'

What Makes It Special

Red Wine: Smooth and full-bodied
Minimal Spice: Balanced warmth with just a hint of edge
Apple Jam: Sweet and subtle mountain touch
Black Pepper: Just enough to wake the flavour
No Sugar Overload, No Frills—Just Accidental Brilliance

Ingredients
(Spiced, Simple, and Satisfying)

- 500 ml red wine
- 1-2 strips orange peel
- 1 cinnamon stick + 2 cloves
- 1 tbsp apple jam
- A pinch of fresh cracked black pepper
- 1 tbsp honey
- Optional: Small splash of water if the wine is bold
- Garnish: Orange slice or cinnamon stick

How to Make It
(Over Fire or Stove)

1. In a saucepan, combine all ingredients except honey.
2. Warm gently over low heat for 10-15 minutes.
3. Do not boil—just let the spices infuse.
4. Taste; add honey if it needs a soft roundness.
5. Strain into mugs, breathe in deeply, and sip slowly.

THE FINAL SIP

Sometimes the best things are a little underthought, a little petty, and somehow...exactly right.

50

THE BIKANER SPICE BOMB
A Fiery Tequila Cocktail with Roasted Cumin, Chilli, and Desert Cool

The Story: A Stolen Spirit, Some Wedding Spices, and a Cocktail Born of Boredom

Dev never meant to stay the night.

He was passing through Bikaner on a simple run—five rare agave bottles for a speakeasy in Delhi, tucked into a crate, wrapped in silence. It wasn't glamorous, just precise. He liked it that way. In, out, no dust in his shoes.

But that afternoon, the Thar Desert had other plans.

A sandstorm swept through like it had a score to settle. Visibility dropped to a whisper. The highway vanished. And Dev, stranded and annoyed, found himself parked beside a roadside *dhaba*, somewhere between a wedding party and a weather warning.

He ordered water, sat on a *charpai* under a tarpaulin that flapped like it wanted to leave, and watched the world blur into a burnt-orange haze.

Then the smell hit him—roasted cumin, red chilli, and lime juice, sharp and thick, rolling in from the back kitchen like an invitation and a dare.

He followed it.

Behind the dhaba, amid tandoors and yelling aunties, a cook was dry-roasting spices in wide steel bowls. Dev leaned in. They exchanged a look. Then, casually, Dev pulled out a bottle from his stash, wiped it once on his sleeve, and said, 'Make something. No lassi. Just...fire.'

The cook raised an eyebrow, wiped his palms on his kurta, and got to work.

He crushed a dried red chilli with roasted cumin and fresh lime juice. Added a splash of jaggery syrup—just enough to give it body. Tossed in a few slices of raw cucumber, the local kind, to cool things down before the storm in the glass. And finally, poured in the tequila, stirred it slow, strained it into a steel glass lined with chilli-salt.

No garnish. No fanfare. Dev took a sip. And paused.

It was bold. Bright. Unruly. The roasted cumin gave it smoke, the chilli gave it pace, the lime pulled it into place, and somewhere between fire and finish, the cucumber caught you.

The cook smirked. Dev laughed, surprised even by his own face.

He did not leave that night. Not until the wind calmed and the sky softened.

Before he left, he carved one word into the edge of the spice shelf with a broken corkscrew—SPICE BOMB—and handed over the rest of the bottle.

'Just don't forget the chilli,' he said.

What Makes This Cocktail Special?

Tequila: Clean, agave-forward heat with herbal edges
Roasted cumin: Smoky, earthy depth straight from desert kitchens
Dried Red Chilli: Sharp, fiery character with a dry heat punch
Jaggery Syrup: Rounds the heat and adds desert sweetness
Cucumber: Cooling freshness that keeps things balanced
Chilli-salt Rim: Hits the lips before the drink hits the gut

Ingredients
(Bold, Dry, and Slightly Unhinged)

- 60 ml silver tequila + 20 ml fresh lime juice
- 10 ml jaggery syrup + ½ tsp roasted cumin powder
- 1 small dried red chilli, crushed (or 2 pinches chilli flakes)
- 3-4 slices of fresh cucumber, lightly muddled
- A pinch of black salt
- Ice cubes
- Garnish: None—unless you want a chilli-salt rim or a thin cucumber slice
- Rim (optional): Mix 1:1 red chilli powder and black salt for the glass edge

How to Make It
(Like You Mean It)

1. If rimming your glass, rub a lime wedge around the rim and dip into the chilli-salt mix.
2. In a shaker, muddle the cucumber slices with lime juice and jaggery syrup.
3. Add tequila, crushed red chilli, roasted cumin, and black salt.
4. Fill with ice and shake hard—this drink earns its name.

5. Strain into a chilled steel glass or rocks glass over fresh ice.
6. Sip slowly—this one rolls in waves.

THE FINAL SIP

Spice like a secret.

Smoke like the air before rain.

And a heat that leaves you grinning, wondering what just hit you.

Indian Espresso Martini

51

INDIAN ESPRESSO MARTINI
Filter Coffee Meets Cocktail Hour

The Story: Deadlines, Avalakki, and the Drink That Did Not Know the Rules

Santosh ran a co-working café in Indiranagar.

It was the kind of spot where people pitched fintech apps while chewing on *avalakki bhat*, argued about UI colours over *podi idlis*, and crowd-tested prototypes between two power cuts.

On a rainy Friday, a Dutch investor walked in—wired, jet-lagged, and unimpressed.

'Espresso martini?' she asked, more demand than question.

Santosh froze.

The espresso machine was dead. Grinder had shorted.

All he had was a tall steel tumbler of Chikmagalur filter coffee decoction, brewed strong and forgotten beside a plate of *rava vada*.

But he had bar instincts.

He grabbed a shaker, poured in the filter coffee, added a shot of vodka, a splash of coffee liqueur, a spoon of brown sugar syrup from the cold brew station, and a dusting of cardamom from the masala shelf.

Shook it with the same energy he used to chase unpaid invoices.

The drink came out dark and glossy, with that signature crema swirl. It smelled like Sunday mornings and smelled like startup survival all at once.

She took one sip.

Eyes widened.

Smile followed.

By Monday, three angel investors were asking,

'Can we get that...filter martini thing?'
And Santosh?
He still hasn't fixed the espresso machine.

What Makes This Cocktail Special?

South Indian Filter Coffee: Bold, rich, aromatic
Vodka + Coffee Liqueur: Classic foundation, now deeply desi
Brown Sugar Syrup: Smooth sweetness with café-bar vibe
Cardamom: Adds a soft whisper of spice that lingers
No Espresso, No Problem: It's all about the decoction

Ingredients
(Creamy, Caffeinated, and Confident)

- 45 ml vodka
- 30 ml strong South Indian filter coffee decoction, chilled
- 15 ml coffee liqueur (like Kahlúa or Indian alternative)
- 10 ml brown sugar syrup (1:1 brown sugar and hot water, cooled)
- A pinch of ground cardamom (optional, but signature)
- Ice cubes
- Garnish: 3 coffee beans or a dusting of cardamom powder

How to Make It
(Shaken, Not Stirred)

1. In a cocktail shaker, combine vodka, chilled filter coffee, coffee liqueur, brown sugar syrup, and cardamom.
2. Fill the shaker with ice and shake hard for 15-20 seconds.
3. Strain into a chilled martini or coupe glass.
4. Garnish with coffee beans or a gentle dusting of cardamom.

THE FINAL SIP

Like a Bengaluru brainstorm: Strong, a little sweet, and best served before deadlines.

52

KOKUM GIN SOUR

Tart, Frothy, and Coastal Cool

The Story: A Bar with No Lemons, a Guest with Expectations, and a Cocktail That Knew the Backwaters

Mihir wasn't the hotel's star bartender.

He wasn't even on the cocktail menu staff.

He just worked the late shift at a boutique resort near Ganpatipule, where the sea met the cliffs and the bar stayed half-empty once the sun dipped.

On most nights, he made gin and tonics for honeymooners and shandies for sleepy families. But that Friday, a woman in a crumpled linen shirt and chef's apron walked in just after 9 p.m.—alone, unreadable, and clearly not there for beach drinks.

She sat down, looked around, then said without blinking:

'Make me something sour. No lime. No lemon. Surprise me.'

Mihir hesitated.

The bar had no imported citrus. The lime stock was gone. The kitchen was on break. He could've said no.

But instead, he opened the cooler and spotted a half bottle of kokum extract, pushed to the back beside the pickles—deep red, syrupy, tart, and quietly brilliant.

He grabbed the gin.

Poured in a measure of kokum.

Added a touch of jaggery syrup for sweetness.

He knew it needed lift—something smooth and silky—but he had no egg white. And this woman did not strike him as someone who'd appreciate shortcuts.

Just then, from the pass-through kitchen counter, he spotted a steel bowl of soaked chickpeas—prepped for tomorrow's misal.

And there it was. The idea.

He ladled out a spoon of the chickpea brine—aquafaba—tossed it into the shaker with the kokum, gin, syrup, and ice, and shook it hard. Twice. One dry shake, one with ice.

He strained it into a chilled coupe glass, the head rising like soft sea foam.

The colour was dusky pink, almost ceremonial. The aroma was botanical and wild.

She took one sip. Then another... Then raised her eyes.

'This tastes like someone made a sour cocktail while watching the monsoon hit a mango orchard,' she said, smiling—not with praise, but recognition.

Mihir just nodded, heart thumping.

'It's kokum,' he said. 'The citrus you forgot about.'

What Makes This Cocktail Special?

Kokum: Naturally sour, floral, and coastal-native
Gin: Botanical, herbaceous base that complements kokum beautifully
Jaggery Syrup: Earthy sweetness to soften the tart edges
Aquafaba (Chickpea Brine): Plant-based froth enhancer for that creamy head—no citrus, no eggs, no apologies

Ingredients
(Elegant, Tangy, and Silky Smooth)

- 50 ml dry gin
- 25 ml kokum syrup or extract
- 15 ml jaggery syrup
- 20 ml aquafaba (chickpea brine, from a can or home-soaked)
- Ice cubes
- Garnish: Dried kokum slice or edible flower (optional)

How to Make It
(Frothy Like a Storm-cloud)

1. In a shaker, add gin, kokum syrup, jaggery syrup, and aquafaba.
2. Dry shake (without ice) for 10–15 seconds to activate the froth.
3. Add ice and shake again for another 10–15 seconds until cold and creamy.
4. Strain into a chilled coupe or sour glass.
5. Let the head settle, admire the dusky pink hue, and sip like the sea's watching.

THE FINAL SIP

It's not a sour for noise.

It's a quiet cocktail that rewrites its own rules—no citrus, no fluff, just tart waves and velvet hush.

Cardamom and Vanilla Bourbon Smash

53

CARDAMOM AND VANILLA BOURBON SMASH

The Train Pantry Experiment

The Story: A Fog Delay, a Pocket Flask, and a Smash That Found Its Rhythm

Arnav did not plan to mix cocktails on a train.

He was a bartender between jobs, between cities, and—as of 8:42 p.m.—between train stations. The overnight express from Lucknow to Mumbai had ground to a halt somewhere past Jhansi, swallowed whole by a winter fog so thick you could not see the chaiwala's shadow.

Wrapped in his scarf and pacing the dimly lit coach, Arnav wandered toward the pantry car just to stretch his legs. That's when he spotted the stash: cardamom pods, a pack of half-broken vanilla biscuits, and a large thermos of boiling water.

One of the pantry boys was humming old Kishore Kumar tunes while trying to make a toast-and-butter sandwich with a blunt knife.

'Got anything stronger than chai?' Arnav asked.

The pantry boy laughed. 'Only if you've got something to trade.'

Arnav reached into his duffle and pulled out a small hip flask of cheap bourbon—'for emergencies,' he joked.

That night counted.

They brewed cardamom tea in a steel jug, crushed a vanilla biscuit into syrup with hot water, and shook the concoction with bourbon and a few mint leaves they found in the dry ration box.

They did not even have ice—just stirred it over a frozen

bottle of mineral water someone had stashed under the luggage rack.

When they poured it into paper chai cups, the coach fell quiet for the first time that night.

Smooth. Spiced. Unexpectedly elegant.

A bourbon smash born between fog horns and footboard gossip.

By morning, when the train started moving again, Arnav had scribbled the recipe on the back of an IRCTC bill and handed it to the pantry boy with a wink.

'Call it what you want,' he said.

'But tell them it was made at mile marker 213, with no ticket, no garnish, and no regrets.'

What Makes This Cocktail Special?

Bourbon: Bold, warm, with smoky undertones that tie it all together

Cardamom: Soft spice that lifts the drink and adds train pantry nostalgia

Vanilla Biscuit Syrup: Invented out of necessity, now the secret weapon

Mint Leaves: Adds freshness and balance No citrus, no fancy garnish–just flavour, humour, and a rumble of wheels beneath you

Ingredients
(Warm, Improvised, and Deliciously Drinkable)

- 60 ml bourbon
- 15 ml vanilla biscuit syrup
- (made by crushing 1 vanilla biscuit into 30 ml hot water, stir until thick and strain)
- 1/4 tsp crushed cardamom seeds (freshly bruised for best flavour)
- 4-5 mint leaves (gently torn)

- Optional: A few dashes of aromatic bitters (if not on a moving train)
- Crushed ice or chilled water bottle for stirring
- Garnish: A mint sprig or half a biscuit (if the pantry did not eat it)

How to Make It

(Pantry Car or Home Bar)

1. Make your vanilla biscuit syrup by combining a biscuit with hot water; mash well, stir, strain and let cool.
2. In a shaker or steel glass, muddle cardamom seeds and mint lightly.
3. Add bourbon, biscuit syrup, and bitters (if using).
4. Add crushed ice or stir it cold over a bottle chilled in your fridge.
5. Strain into a steel tumbler or lowball glass.
6. No garnish needed, but a broken vanilla biscuit on the side won't hurt.

THE FINAL SIP

It's spice with steam, sweet with soul, and proof that great cocktails can come from fog delays and chai thermoses.

54

PAAN MOJITO

A Colonial Sip of India

The Story: The Dutch Bride, a Bungalow Evening, and Her First Real Taste of India

Pondicherry, 1941. The shutters creaked open just past sunrise. Elise had been in India for three weeks, and every day smelled like tamarind trees, damp stone, and the pages of old letters.

Her husband, Captain Willem van Rijn, had been posted here to manage Dutch trade interests. She had arrived on a ship two months after the wedding—hopeful, pale, curious—and found herself mostly confined to a whitewashed bungalow that looked out over the Bay of Bengal.

He was always away. Reports. Meetings. Maps. Silk. Salt.

One evening, under a linen fan and thick air, she turned to him and said, 'You promised me India, not paperwork.'

The next afternoon, he finally obliged.

They left the compound, stepping into the rhythmic hum of the city—markets loud with spice and smell, sea breeze laced with fried plantains, streets pulsing with life far more vivid than anything inside their walled bungalow.

He led her down a narrow street, through a brass-studded door, into a small local tavern filled with laughter and smoke. It wasn't in any colonial directory.

Willem said nothing. Just nodded to the barman—a wiry man with a white scarf and a betel-stained grin—who brought over two clay tumblers.

Mint. Lime. Crushed ice. A swirl of gulkand.

Betel leaf, muddled rough.

And clear local spirit, poured like an afterthought.

Elise blinked at the drink. It smelled like perfume and rain.

She sipped. And paused. Then smiled. Wide. Unfiltered. India.

It was bold and sweet and sharp—like poetry after rules.

She turned to Willem—'Now this,' she said, 'is what I married you for.'

The barman laughed. Called it his *'paan ka sharbat for the sahebs.'*

Elise never forgot the taste.

Years later, in a quieter country, she would try to replicate it with mint, rum, and paan essence. It was never quite right.

But that moment—India, her husband, the drink—remained bottled inside her, forever fizzy.

What Makes This Cocktail Special?

Betel Leaf (Paan): Bold, aromatic, herbaceous twist on the classic mint
Gulkand: Sweet floral rose jam that balances the green sharpness
Mint and Lime: Mojito core with Indian flavour bridge
White Rum: Crisp spirit that lets the ingredients shine
Soda: Brings the fizz and keeps it light

Ingredients
(Fragrant, Sweet, and Inviting)

- 60 ml white rum + 2-3 fresh betel leaves, torn into small pieces
- 10-12 mint leaves + 20 ml fresh lime juice
- 10 ml gulkand
- 10 ml simple syrup
- 60-90 ml soda water
- Ice cubes

- Garnish: Rolled betel leaf, mint sprig, or dried rose petal

How to Make It
(Shaken or Built in Glass)

1. In a shaker or sturdy glass, muddle betel leaves, mint, lime juice, gulkand, and syrup.
2. Add white rum and fill with ice.
3. Shake or stir vigorously to mix the ingredients.
4. Strain into a tall glass over fresh ice and top with soda water and give a light stir.
5. Garnish and serve chilled.

THE FINAL SIP

It's paan after dinner.
It's mojito before the sun sets.
It's tradition, kissed by rebellion.

55

THE CHAAT MASALA BLOODY MARY
Delhi's Loudest Cocktail

The Story: A Speakeasy, Some Snark, and the Masala That Shut Them Up

Aarav did not go to bartending school.

He learned pouring by watching uncles mix Old Monk with Limca behind wedding tents. His cocktail education came from *paanwala* hacks and hostel jugaad—not Paris, not London.

But somehow, he found himself running the bar at 'Blank,' a dimly lit Delhi speakeasy with too much neon and not enough salt.

Every Friday, the orders were the same:

'Negroni, but authentic.'

'Bloody Mary, but don't mess with it.'

Imported tomato juice. Tabasco from a plastic bottle. Worcestershire if the barback remembered.

Aarav snapped one night.

He grabbed the shaker, looked the suited guy straight in the eye, and said:

'You want classic? Try Chandni Chowk style.'

He muddled fresh green chilli, added a pinch of chaat masala, kala namak, a squeeze of desi nimbu, and shook it with vodka and homemade tomato pulp thick enough to hold a spoon.

He poured it over ice in a steel tumbler.

No celery. No olive. Just a slice of cucumber and a rim dusted with *lal mirch*.

The critic smirked. Sipped. Paused. Blinked.

Then emptied the glass.

The Chaat Masala Bloody Mary

Two nights later, food blogs called it 'the cocktail with attitude.'

A month later, it was Delhi's most-ordered brunch drink.

Aarav did not rename it.

He just added a note on the menu:

'Not your gora uncle's Bloody Mary.'

What Makes This Cocktail Special?

Fresh Tomato Pulp: Richer, thicker, fuller than any bottled juice

Chaat Masala + Kala Namak: Desi umami bombs

Green Chilli: Brings fresh heat without overpowering

Desi Lemon: Adds brightness and balance

Cucumber Garnish: Keeps it cool amidst the fire

Ingredients
(Savory, Spicy, and Delhi-Slick)

- 60 ml vodka
- 90 ml fresh tomato pulp or thick tomato juice
- 1/2 tsp chaat masala + a pinch of kala namak
- 1 small green chilli, finely chopped or muddled
- 10 ml fresh lemon juice
- A dash of black pepper
- Ice cubes
- Garnish: Cucumber spear or chilli-salt rim (optional)

How to Make It
(Like Aarav Would)

1. In a shaker, combine green chilli, lemon juice, and a pinch of kala namak.
2. Add tomato pulp, chaat masala, vodka, and ice.
3. Shake hard and fast—this drink has no patience.
4. Strain into a tall steel or glass tumbler filled with ice.

5. Garnish with cucumber or keep it bare and bold.
6. Optional: Rim glass with red chilli + salt mix for extra punch.

THE FINAL SIP

It's brunch in Delhi. With masala.

With fire. With absolutely no apologies.

56

OVERRIPE MANGO RUM PUNCH

Sweetness Saved, Not Wasted

The Story: Goa's First No-Waste Cocktail Festival and the Drink That Won without Even Trying

Goa had hosted raves, yoga retreats, EDM sunsets, and silent discos—but this was a first.

A No-Waste Cocktail Festival—an idea hatched by a few eco-bartenders, supported by local cafés, and backed by some scrappy zero-waste startups—was set to shake things up on a Sunday that smelled like salt, ambition, and leftover fruit.

Cafés from Arambol to Palolem showed up.

The rule? Use what's about to be wasted.

No imported juices. No flashy garnishes.

Just kitchen scraps, rejected produce, and creative hustle.

At the back of the event, behind a surf shack with reggae thumping and kids chasing beach dogs, Ravi stood over a plastic crate of mangoes—half-squished, speckled, days past their shelf life.

'Trash,' someone said. He raised an eyebrow. 'Treasure.'

He scooped the pulp—syrupy, golden, intensely ripe—into a steel pot.

Added white rum, a squeeze of fresh lime, a glug of jaggery syrup, and a pinch of sea salt.

Then came the coconut water, chilled overnight in a freezer that barely worked.

A few torn mint leaves. One big stir.

No machines. No labels. Just flavour. And flow.

He poured the punch into reused coconut shells and handed them out with zero marketing, no hype.

By late afternoon, his stall was empty.

Not one mango wasted. Not one punch untouched.

The judges?

Did not care about garnish. They tasted sunlight, skin, pulp, and Goa in a cup.

Ravi did not win a trophy.

But someone asked if he could franchise the recipe.

What Makes This Cocktail Special?

Overripe Mangoes: Instead of tossing them, you celebrate their peak sweetness and soft richness

Jaggery Syrup: Adds depth and earthiness, no refined sugar needed

Coconut Water: Naturally cooling and refreshing, the perfect light balance

Mint and Sea Salt: Punch up flavour while keeping the palate fresh

Low-waste by Design: No waste, no compromise, and every sip tells a story

Ingredients
(Tropical, Tangy, and Totally Upcycled)

- 100 ml overripe mango pulp (ripe to the edge of mushy)
- 60 ml white rum
- 20 ml fresh lime juice
- 15 ml jaggery syrup (1:1 jaggery + warm water, cooled)
- 60-90 ml coconut water, chilled
- 6-8 fresh mint leaves, lightly torn
- A pinch of sea salt
- Ice cubes
- Garnish: Mango peel curl or mint sprig (optional but pretty)

How to Make It
(Festival-Ready, Cooler-Pour Friendly)

1. Scoop mango pulp into a mixing bowl or shaker.
2. Add lime juice, jaggery syrup, mint leaves, and a pinch of salt.
3. Pour in the rum and give it a vigorous shake (or stir in a big batch bowl).
4. Add chilled coconut water and stir gently.
5. Pour into chilled glasses, coconut shells, or mason jars.
6. Top with a garnish—or skip it, like Ravi.

THE FINAL SIP

This drink did not win a medal.

It won the moment.

And that's all mangoes ever wanted.

57

JACKFRUIT SEED OLD-FASHIONED

Legacy in a Glass

The Story: A Forest Ranger's Will, a Hidden Envelope, and a Cocktail to Remember

When the lawyer read the will, Nikhil did not expect much. His grandfather, Hari Rao, had spent the last thirty years as a forest ranger in the Western Ghats—more leaves in his life than legal documents.

But right after the house and books and boots were listed, came a curious line:

'To my grandson, I leave my most trusted ritual.

You'll find it in the steel spice box under the stone grinder.

Use it only when the world feels too loud.'

Nikhil flew to Agumbe a week later. The cottage sat wrapped in silence, just as he remembered from childhood: the smell of wet mud, turmeric, and firewood smoke. He found the box—dented, old, exactly where the will had said—and inside, tucked beneath dried peppercorns and bay leaves, was an envelope.

In his grandfather's unmistakable, tight lettering:

'When you miss the smell of earth after rain, make this.'

It was a drink. Not fancy. But thoughtful.

A Jackfruit Seed Old-Fashioned—a ritual born from decades of field patrol, temple feasts, and monsoon solitude.

Roasted jackfruit seed syrup.

A shot of smoky Indian whiskey.

Jaggery, not sugar.

Bitters made from forest bark.

No garnish. No glass rims. Just wisdom and warmth in a tumbler.

That night, Nikhil followed the recipe exactly.

He crushed the seeds in the same mortar. Simmered the jaggery syrup over a wood flame. Stirred the drink slowly.

When he took a sip, the flavour hit like a memory: earth, smoke, quiet strength.

He sat on the veranda as cicadas chirped and the jungle exhaled.

His grandfather hadn't left him money.

He had left him a ritual, a recipe, a way to come back home whenever he needed.

What Makes This Cocktail Special?

Jackfruit Seeds: Upcycled, roasted, and rich with nutty undertones
Jaggery Syrup: Dark, earthy sweetness with no refined sugar
Smoky Indian Whiskey: Adds fire and depth to every sip
Sustainably Soulful: Born from tradition, forest wisdom, and zero waste
Handwritten into a Will: It's not just a drink, it's a message across time

Ingredients
(Earthy, Bold, and Legacy-Worthy)

- 60 ml smoky Indian whiskey (a local single malt)
- 15 ml jackfruit seed-infused jaggery syrup (see below)
- 2 dashes aromatic bitters
- Ice (a single large cube preferred)
- Garnish: Roasted jackfruit seed or nothing at all

To Make the Jackfruit Seed Syrup

1. Roast 8–10 peeled jackfruit seeds until golden
2. Crack them lightly and simmer with 3 tbsp jaggery in 1 cup water
3. Let steep 30 minutes, strain, and cool
4. Store chilled for up to a week

How to Make the Cocktail

1. Combine whiskey, syrup, and bitters in a mixing glass.
2. Add ice and stir for 20 seconds.
3. Strain into a rocks glass over fresh ice.
4. Take your time. This is not a city drink.

THE FINAL SIP

This isn't just heritage.
It's how a forest man said,
'I remember you.'

58

PICKLED MANGO MARTINI

The Home Chef's Sour Revolution

The Story: A Ring Light, a Recipe Rebellion, and a Martini with Bite

For three years, Geetanjali was known for her pastel-perfect food blog.

'Glow Bowls,' 'Bliss Laddoos,' 'Detox Dals'.

Clean eating. Minimal garnish. Everything air-fried.

Her audience? Huge.

Her kitchen? Sponsored.

Her mom? Sceptical.

'You'll eventually want real flavour,' her mom would say, stirring something oily and glorious on the stove. Geetanjali would just smile–until one Thursday afternoon.

She was prepping for a collab shoot with a cold-pressed juice brand. The tripod was up, the oat milk frother humming, when she saw it:

A leftover jar of mango pickle, half-full, hiding behind the kombucha bottles.

The lid was crusted. The brine looked angry.

And her mom's label read:

'Not for weak tastebuds.'

She opened it. Sniffed. Smiled.

'Screw it.'

Tanya scrapped the detox spritz.

Grabbed her Indian craft gin, a wedge of lime, and spooned in a dollop of that aged mango pulp. She added a splash of the brine, a pinch of crushed chilli flakes, and shook it like she meant it.

She poured the drink into a frosted martini glass, hit record, and went live:

'Today, we're making chaos. And calling it a martini.'

The comments rolled in:

'WHAT??'

'Wait, did she say achar??'

'IS THIS LEGAL?'

By midnight, she had 40K shares and a new hashtag trending:

#SourRevolution

Her audience did not just love it—they begged for more.

She pinned the recipe and wrote:

'We were taught to tone it down. But flavour doesn't need a filter.'

—Love, Mom's Daughter (and her pickle jar)

What Makes This Cocktail Special?

Achar Pulp: Funky, spicy, and bold—no sugarcoating
Pickle Brine Splash: Adds depth, salt, and tang

Craft Gin: Floral and botanical base to balance the heat
Lime Juice: Brightens the sour notes
Unexpected, Unforgettable: A martini that speaks loud, proud, and very desi

Ingredients
(Sharp, Spiced, and Fearless)

- 50 ml botanical-forward Indian gin
- 1 tsp mashed mango pickle pulp
- 10 ml mango pickle brine
- 15 ml fresh lime juice
- Pinch of chilli flakes or crushed mustard seeds (optional)
- Ice cubes
- Garnish: Thin dried mango slice or just a chilli salt rim

How to Make It
(Desi Shaken, Not Stirred)

1. In a shaker, add gin, lime juice, pickle pulp, and brine.
2. Add chilli flakes (if using) and ice.
3. Shake vigorously for at least 30 seconds to emulsify.
4. Double strain into a chilled martini glass.
5. Rim the glass with chilli salt if you are feeling dramatic.

THE FINAL SIP

It's loud. It's sharp.
It's not here to be polite.
It's the cocktail version of 'I told you so.'

59

FERMENTED PINEAPPLE AND TODDY SMASH

The Accidental Coastal Hero

The Story: A Crate, a Niece, and a Tropical Mistake That Changed Summer

It started with a forgotten crate.

In a sleepy coastal village near Ratnagiri, the sun showed no mercy that week. The fruit stall sizzled under a tattered blue tarp, and Manohar Bhau, the local pineapple vendor, was too busy selling mangoes to notice the pile of fruit sweating under the table.

Two days later, his niece Reva, home from her food science course in Pune, was helping him clean the stall. She lifted a half-sunk pineapple out of the crate and sniffed.

Fizzy. Sweet. Tangy. Almost...sparkly.

'Bhau, this isn't spoiled,' she said. 'It's *perfectly fermented.*'

He squinted. 'Spoiled is spoiled. Throw it.'

Reva did not. Instead, she juiced it into a steel bowl, added a splash of fresh toddy from the neighbour's tree, a squeeze of lime, a pinch of red chilli salt, and a few crushed curry leaves.

No shaker. Just her hands and instinct.

She served it over ice in an old pickle jar. It fizzed like a monsoon storm, smelled like every Konkan summer she had ever known.

They both sipped. Paused. Grinned.

The next day, she added it–unofficially–to the menu as *Fizzy Pine*.

Within a week, the tiny stall had tourists asking for the 'drink that tastes like sunshine and rebellion.'

Bhau still calls it 'that spoiled thing.' Reva calls it 'my final year project.'

Everyone else just calls it the best thing to happen to summer since saltwater breeze.

What Makes This Cocktail Special?

Naturally Fermented Pineapple: Bright, sour-sweet, with natural fizz

Fresh Coconut Toddy: Lightly alcoholic, earthy, and traditionally coastal

Chilli-lime Salt: Adds zing (mix of rock salt, chilli powder, lime zest)

Low-waste, Local, Genius: Born by accident, perfected with instinct

Ingredients
(Fizzy, Funky and Fresh)

- 90 ml fermented pineapple juice
- 60 ml fresh coconut toddy/neera (chilled)
- 10 ml lime juice + 1 pinch chilli-lime salt
- 3-4 fresh curry leaves, lightly crushed
- Ice cubes
- Garnish: Pineapple wedge and curry leaf float

How to Make It
(Village Jugaad Meets Modern Cool)

1. In a steel or clay mixing cup, combine pineapple juice, toddy, and lime juice.
2. Add chilli salt and crushed curry leaves.
3. Stir gently with a spoon—don't over-shake or kill the fizz.
4. Pour over ice in a tall glass or terracotta cup.
5. Garnish with a fresh pineapple wedge and curry leaf.
6. Serve cold, barefoot optional.

THE FINAL SIP

It's fermentation by accident. Invention by instinct. And summer in a sip.

60

CARROT AND GINGER VODKA MULE
The Trackside Mule Gets Wheels

The Story: A Bus Stand, a Halwa Pot, and the Cocktail Nobody Saw Coming

The bus to Nainital was already 45 minutes late.

The team from MangoTree Advertising stood in various stages of sleep-deprived disarray outside the Haldwani bus stand—coffee-starved, deadline-drained, but pretending this was a 'retreat.'

Their creative director, Arjun, had insisted they unplug.

'Let the hills inspire you,' he said.

But the only thing inspiring anyone that morning was the smell of carrot halwa bubbling from the tea vendor's stall.

As the steam curled up from chipped aluminium pots, a bright orange heap of grated carrot was scooped out and tossed near the stove—leftovers from the morning batch.

One of the younger copywriters, Gauri, a low-key cocktail nerd and self-proclaimed 'flavour hacker,' nudged the tea vendor.

'Bhaiya, can I borrow some of that?'

He raised an eyebrow but handed her a ladle.

She rummaged through the team's retreat snack bag,

found a bottle of vodka, fresh ginger, and a lime someone packed for motion sickness.

From the vendor's own kit, she borrowed soda and a pinch of black salt.

She smashed the carrot and ginger with a spoon, stirred in vodka and lime in a steel glass, and topped it with soda—no shaker, no garnish, just pure chaos and instinct.

'Try this,' she said, handing it to Arjun.

He took a sip.

Paused.

Looked around and said,

'This. This is our tagline now.'

Everyone demanded a taste.

Within minutes, the ad team was crowded around the tea stall, sipping versions of the drink from paper cups, trying to name it.

The tea vendor finally chuckled and said,

'Track pe toh nahi ho...par yeh ek dum mule jaisa lagta hai.'

And just like that, the Trackside Mule rolled into cocktail legend.

No ice. No bar tools.

Just a halwa mistake, a roadside stall, and a story better than the agency's next campaign.

What Makes This Cocktail Special?

Leftover Grated Carrot: Juicy, earthy, sweet—a zero-waste win

Crushed Fresh Ginger: Spicy punch with desi warmth

Vodka Base: Neutral spirit that lets the produce shine

Soda + Lime: Keeps it light and fizzy, travel-friendly

Made with Scraps, Soul, and Steel Glasses: No garnish required

Ingredients
(Bright, Rooty, and Roadside-Inspired)

- 45 ml vodka
- 2 tbsp fresh grated carrot (leftover or juiced pulp)
- 1 tsp crushed fresh ginger + 15 ml fresh lime juice
- 90 ml soda water
- Pinch of black salt or chaat masala (optional)
- Ice cubes (optional if served fresh)
- Garnish: None required—but a carrot shaving or lime slice if you are feeling fancy

How to Make It
(Bus Stop Style)

1. In a steel or glass tumbler, mash grated carrot and ginger with lime juice.
2. Add vodka and a pinch of black salt.
3. Fill with soda and stir gently.
4. Add ice if available, or serve it cold and raw, just like the story.
5. Share. Because this drink doesn't work alone.

THE FINAL SIP

A roadside crush.

A carrot with kick.

Proof that sometimes, the best cocktail starts with a bus delay.

61

GREEN APPLE JALJEERA SPRITZ

The Secret That Stole the Shaadi

The Story: A Bridal Sip, a Masi's Discovery, and the Cocktail That Went Viral

It was 44 degrees in Jaipur.

The kind of heat that turned petals limp and made aunties whisper 'AC nahi lagaya?' while fanning themselves with mehendi menus.

In the middle of the chaos, Naina, the bride's best friend–and known cocktail troublemaker–stood guard near the drinks table, unimpressed.

The options were tragic: sugary sodas, melting syrups, and a mocktail called 'Minty Sunshine.'

She rolled her eyes. Quietly, she pulled out a zip pouch from her sling:

Fresh green apple slices. A tiny bottle of white rum. Homemade jaljeera spice in a film canister. And a can of club soda she had smuggled past the hotel's 'no outside food' rule.

She whispered to the bride: 'One sip. Nobody needs to know.'

She muddled the apple, added the spice and rum, topped it with lime and soda, and handed over a steel cup with a wink.

The bride sipped. Her eyes widened. She looked at Naina.

'What *is* this sorcery?'

Just then, her Masi, the infamous family watchdog, walked by and said,

'Beta, what's this churan-flavoured nimbu pani you are hiding?'

Before Naina could intercept, Masi took a sip.

And froze. *'Zara ek aur do,'* she muttered, already signaling the caterer to fetch a tray.

By sundown, the Green Apple Jaljeera Spritz had spread through the venue like baraati gossip.

No one knew what was in it, but aunties were asking if it was 'good for digestion.'

Uncles were adding extra soda and calling it 'chilled achar punch.'

By the time the bride walked into her sangeet, people were sipping her secret like it was part of the menu.

Naina?

She did not mind. She just muttered under her breath:

'I only make cocktails that start small—and end viral.'

What Makes This Cocktail Special?

Fresh Green Apple: Tart, juicy, vibrant

Jaljeera Spice Mix: Tangy, salty, deeply Indian

White Rum (or Gin/Vodka): Clean spirit with room for flavour play

Lime + Soda: Keeps it light and crushable

Perfect for Heat, Humidity, and *Haldi* Ceremonies

Ingredients
(Sharp, Spiced and Sangeet-Ready)

- 45 ml white rum (vodka or gin also works)
- 1/2 green apple, diced or thinly sliced
- 1/2 tsp jaljeera powder
- 15 ml fresh lime juice + 90–120 ml chilled club soda
- Pinch of black salt
- Ice cubes
- Garnish: Thin green apple slice, mint sprig, or even a chilli-lime rim if you are feeling filmi

How to Make It
(Secretly or Boldly)

1. In a shaker or sturdy glass, muddle the green apple with lime juice and jaljeera powder.
2. Add rum and a pinch of black salt if using.
3. Shake gently with ice, or stir if you are using a steel cup and working undercover.
4. Strain into a tall glass filled with ice (or a paper cup if you are in disguise).
5. Top with chilled soda.
6. Garnish with a green apple slice or mint.
7. Whisper it to the bride. Let masi discover it herself.

THE FINAL SIP

A secret sip turned show-stealer. Masala meets fizz. Tart, sharp, and gossip-proof.

Just the kind of drink that'll be remembered longer than the couple's first dance.

Bengali Gondhoraj Gimlet

62

BENGALI GONDHORAJ GIMLET

The Jalpaiguri Bungalow Secret

The Story: A Locked Trunk, a Fragrant Letter, and the Gimlet That Waited 63 Years

The rains in Jalpaiguri don't fall.

They arrive like old guests–slow, deliberate, unapologetically damp.

When Rhea Mitra inherited her grandfather's overgrown bungalow just outside the Dooars forest line, she found it full of dust, mothballs, and letters.

Most of the house was untouched–furniture draped in cotton sheets, calendars frozen in the 1970s, and one steel trunk bound shut with a rusted lock.

When it finally clicked open, it wasn't gold or antiques inside.

Just a bundle of fragrant dried Gondhoraj limes, a tin of British gin wrapped in old newspaper, and a folded envelope marked in elegant Bengali script: 'For the day you forgive her.'

Rhea knew the story: Her grandfather, a retired forest conservator, had once fallen in love with a woman from Kolkata.

The family hadn't approved. She left, quietly. He stayed, stubborn.

But she had once visited–just once–in the monsoon of 1959, and left this recipe behind.

Gondhoraj juice, a touch of cordial, and gin–shaken gently and sipped slowly. She called it 'fragrance in a glass.'

Rhea, moved by the scent and the silence, made it that same night.

She crushed a fresh Gondhoraj from the garden tree,

added local gin from Siliguri, and recreated the gimlet by oil-lamp glow.

It wasn't a drink. It was a message.

And somehow, it made the house feel less abandoned.

Now, every August, on the night the rain returns, Rhea lights a candle in the veranda, makes the gimlet, and raises a glass to the recipe that waited six decades to be poured.

What Makes This Cocktail Special?

Gondhoraj Lime: Fragrant, citrusy, uniquely Bengali
Indian Gin: Clean, botanical base
Simple Syrup or Lime Cordial: Light sweetness to carry the lime
A Sip that Feels like a Letter Never Sent: Emotional, elegant, unforgettable

Ingredients
(Rainy, Aromatic, and Lightly Melancholic)

- 50 ml botanical Indian gin
- 20 ml fresh Gondhoraj lime juice + 15 ml simple syrup or sweet lime cordial
- Optional: Dash of soda for a modern twist
- Ice cubes
- Garnish: A thin Gondhoraj peel twist or dried lime chip

How to Make It
(Quiet and Scented)

1. Combine gin, lime juice, and syrup in a shaker with ice.
2. Shake gently—don't bruise the scent.
3. Strain into a coupe or small tumbler.
4. Garnish with Gondhoraj peel.
5. Sip where the breeze can reach you.

THE FINAL SIP

This is not a cocktail. It's a rain-drenched memory and a lime that waited half a century to be tasted.

63

KOLHAPURI FIRECRACKER

The Chef's Day Off

The Story: Misal, Madness, and a Glass of Burnt Gold

By 9:30 p.m., the Kolhapur Food Mahotsav had wound down.

The last plates of *misal pav* were cleared.

The chutneys had crusted.

The smoke from the tandoor clung to the kitchen like a second skin.

Chef Vivek, who'd just cooked 400 orders in one day, leaned against the walk-in fridge and finally exhaled.

His sous-chef, Sameer, collapsed on a crate of tomatoes, laughing.

'You know what we need?' 'A month off?'

'No. A drink that tastes like today.' Vivek smirked.

He had something better. He reached for the back shelf—where he had hidden his favourite post-service fix for years.

A slab of jaggery. A dried Kolhapuri mirchi. Tamarind pulp. And a bottle of smoky Indian whiskey.

In a small steel pot, he melted the jaggery and steeped the chilli in it till the air itself felt red-hot.

He added a splash of tamarind, a glug of whiskey, and

stirred it all with a battered steel spoon.

No garnish. No glassware. Just sweat, silence, and spice.

They sipped from chai cups, still wearing aprons stained with turmeric and mirchi oil... Sameer coughed once. Then smiled.

'This isn't a drink, Chef. This is a firecracker.'

By the time the rest of the kitchen staff joined, Vivek was already on batch two.

It never made it to the menu.

But that night, in the back kitchen of a festival that fed thousands, a legend was poured—one hot, jaggery-slicked glass at a time.

What Makes This Cocktail Special?

Toasted Kolhapuri Chilli: Not just heat, but flavour
Jaggery Syrup: Earthy, rich, and kitchen-authentic
Tamarind: Tartness that cuts through the fire
Indian Whiskey: Smoked, grounded, bold
Born in a Real Kitchen, Not A Bar: Honest to the bone

Ingredients
(Culinary, Complex, and Pure Grit)

- 60 ml Indian whiskey
- 15 ml jaggery syrup + 10 ml tamarind extract
- 1 dried Kolhapuri red chilli, lightly toasted
- Pinch of smoked salt or kala namak
- Ice cubes
- Garnish: Chilli flake rim or no garnish at all—up to you

How to Make It
(Sweaty, Spicy and Satisfying)

1. In a small saucepan, steep the chilli in warm jaggery syrup for 2-3 minutes.

2. Remove chilli, then stir in tamarind extract and let cool.
3. In a shaker or glass, combine the syrup mix with whiskey and a pinch of smoked salt.
4. Stir gently with ice to chill and dilute.
5. Strain into a steel or ceramic glass—or just a chai cup for truth.
6. Sip. Let the fire rise.

THE FINAL SIP

It burns, then hugs. Like the kitchen after closing.

Loud. Bold. And made with the hands that fed you.

64

ASSAM TEA AND BOURBON SMASH
The Midnight Forest Retreat

The Story: Where Bourbon Met the Jungle's Breath

Just off the floodplain, beyond the elephant tracks of Kaziranga, there's a small eco-lodge that doesn't advertise. No neon, no website. Just a gate draped in hibiscus vines and a hand-carved board that reads:

'Come if you are quiet.'

At the heart of this retreat is a bamboo bar open on all sides—no music, no machines—just the rustling of sal leaves, the steady blink of fireflies, and the heavy breathing of the forest at night.

Ravi, the lodge's in-house mixologist, arrived here on

a six-month sabbatical from a London bar—and never left.

He now wears slippers, speaks Assamese, and refuses to serve anything before 9 p.m.

His signature drink?

Only made after midnight.

He begins by brewing second flush Assam tea—deep and tannic—over slow coals. While it steeps, he muddles fresh roselle petals (locally known as *tenga mora*)—tart and ruby red, hand-plucked by a village woman who brings a bundle every other morning.

Into this, he adds ginger root pounded with the base of a tea glass, a drizzle of forest honey, and a precise pour of aged Indian bourbon he smuggled in from the mainland during his last supply run.

No shaker. Just a tall spoon and intuition.

The lodge guests, mostly artists, conservationists, or couples escaping something, sit barefoot on cane mats, sipping in silence.

When asked what this mystery drink is called, Ravi always says the same thing:

'It's not a drink. It's the jungle exhaling.'

Some say it tastes like midnight fog.

Others say it reminds them of the sound elephants make just before sunrise.

But everyone agrees—it's the only drink that can make time slow down.

And if you are lucky, the night you sip it will end with thunder rolling in from the east and a flame-backed woodpecker calling once—just once—before disappearing into the dark.

What Makes This Cocktail Special?

Second Flush Assam Tea: Dark, bold, reflective
Roselle Petals (Tenga Mora): Tangy, floral, locally foraged

Ginger and Wild Honey: Earthy warmth and layered sweetness
Aged Bourbon: Rich, grounding, and slightly smoky
Steeped in Silence, Served in Whispers

Ingredients
(Wild, Tart, and Deep-Flavoured)

- 60 ml aged Indian bourbon
- 45 ml strong Assam tea
- 15 ml wild honey syrup
- 1 tsp crushed roselle petals
- 5 ml fresh ginger juice or crushed root
- Ice (large cube preferred)
- Garnish: Roselle petal or tiny bay leaf

How to Make It
(Like the Forest Would)

1. Brew strong second flush Assam tea, let it cool to room temperature.
2. In a shaker or mixing glass, add crushed roselle petals, ginger, and honey syrup.
3. Add bourbon and tea.
4. Stir slowly over ice—don't rush the chill.
5. Double strain into a clay or heavy-bottomed glass.
6. Garnish with a roselle petal or nothing at all. Serve barefoot if possible.

THE FINAL SIP

It's not poured. It's brewed by breeze.

Tart, warm, and slow like the jungle's own breath.

The kind of cocktail that doesn't ask for attention—it finds you.

65

MALABAR COAST PEPPER MARTINI

The Boatman's Night Off

The Story: Laughter, Liquor, and the Jetty Bar That Never Closed

By sunset, the backwaters had quieted.

The tourists had returned to their cottages, bellies full of appam and stories.

And at the edge of the dock, under a thatched palm roof, Raghavan's boat crew was just getting started.

It was Onam eve, and laughter echoed across the canal as banana leaves rustled with leftover fritters, and a local drum thumped somewhere down the lane. But all eyes were on Raghavan, who had vanished into his small tiled kitchen and hadn't returned.

When he finally walked back, he carried a jug.

'Vodka?' someone teased.

'From that actor fellow last month,' he nodded.

'But this one's different.'

They watched as he poured the mix into steel tumblers—white, creamy, with a scent that was hard to place: a whisper of lime, a memory of spice, and something green and grounding.

He had crushed Tellicherry black pepper straight into the vodka.

Added fresh coconut milk he had strained himself that morning.

Squeezed in a bit of lime, and—without saying much—tucked a small tulsi leaf inside each glass.

'For balance,' he muttered. They lifted their tumblers.

The first sip hit cold, then warm, then sharp.

Cool like the canal. Bold like Onam. And just spicy

enough to start a song.

Vinod let out a cough. Mani's eyes widened. Ramesh raised his glass like it was a trophy.

They did not ask for a name.

But later that night, as they danced barefoot on the jetty to a beat only they could hear, someone called it 'The Silent Storm.'

And that's what it became. Now, every Onam, Raghavan makes that martini again. No recipes, no bar. Just a jug, a laugh, and a memory steeped in spice and salt air.

And when a new boatman joins the crew, the drink is the test.

If he can take the storm in one sip and still smile—he's one of them.

What Makes This Cocktail Special?

Tellicherry Black Pepper: From the spice heartland, it brings bold, floral heat
Fresh Coconut Milk: Smooth and tropical, the soul of Kerala in a pour
Tulsi Leaf: A sacred herb adding calm, depth, and a gentle herbal note
Vodka: Neutral and clean, letting the spice and milk shine through
Born on the Jetty, Not the Menu: This is Kerala's spirit, stirred not scripted

Ingredients
(Spiced, Coastal, and Crowd-Worthy)

- 60 ml vodka
- 30 ml fresh coconut milk
- 10 ml fresh lime juice—adds brightness and lift
- 15 ml jaggery syrup (optional)
- 1/4 tsp freshly crushed Tellicherry black pepper

- 2-3 small tulsi leaf—for aroma and grounding calm
- Ice cubes—to chill and tame the storm

How to Make It (Backwater-Style Simplicity)

1. In a shaker, combine vodka, coconut milk, lime juice, jaggery syrup, and crushed pepper.
2. Add a lightly crushed tulsi leaf—just enough to release its oils.
3. Fill with ice and shake briefly but with confidence.
4. Strain into a chilled steel tumbler or a wide glass.
5. Float a fresh tulsi leaf on top, and let it rest for a second before sipping.

THE FINAL SIP

White as moonlight, warm as festival fire, and spiced like old secrets shared under starlight.

The kind of martini that doesn't belong in a bar—it belongs on a dock, after laughter.

66

UTTARAYAN CITRUS SPRITZ
The Sky, the Rooftop, and a Drink That Rose with the Kites

The Story: The Aunt, the Spritz, and the Loudest Rooftop in Ahmedabad

Every year on January 14th, the rooftops of Ahmedabad transform into a riot of colours, music, and the high-pitched war cry of *'Kaipo che!'*

The Joshi family's terrace was no exception.

Three generations. Two loudspeakers.

And at least seven people yelling at each other about who let the kite fly into the neighbour's mango tree.

At the centre of it all was Baa's sister—Daxa Masi—the one with silver hair, the loudest laugh, and the best drink game in the family.

While the rest of the adults argued over thread reels and chutney proportions, Daxa Masi disappeared into the kitchen and came back with a jug full of sunlight.

She had squeezed fresh oranges, *mosambi*, and a hint of lemon, added a splash of white rum brought by masaji from his last trip to Mumbai, and topped it off with soda water and toasted cumin syrup.

'No cheating,' she said, pouring it into steel tumblers. 'You only get a refill if your kite stays up for more than five minutes!'

The drink was tangy, light, fizzy—and just enough to make the sky look even bluer.

By sundown, Daxa Masi had run out of rum and patience.

So she poured the last glass for herself, raised it to the tangle of kites above, and said: 'They fly high, but I stir better.'

And just like that, the Uttarayan Citrus Spritz became the Joshi family tradition—served every year with kites, tangy snacks, and stories that soared higher than the kites themselves.

What Makes This Cocktail Special?

Seasonal Citrus: Oranges, mosambi, lemon—sunlight in a glass
Toasted Cumin Syrup: Adds warmth and a Gujarati pantry twist
White Rum or Gin: Light spirit that doesn't overpower

Sparkling Soda: The fizz that mimics flight
Born on A Terrace, Made to Toast the Skies

Ingredients
(Zesty, Fizzy, and Kite-Worthy)

- 45 ml white rum (or gin, for a more botanical version)
- 30 ml fresh orange juice
- 20 ml mosambi (sweet lime) juice + 10 ml fresh lemon juice
- 15 ml toasted cumin syrup (see tip below)
- Soda water—to top up
- Ice cubes
- Garnish: Orange wedge and a pinch of toasted cumin seeds

How to Make It
(Terrace-Ready Simplicity)

1. In a shaker, combine rum, citrus juices, and toasted cumin syrup.
2. Add ice and give it a light shake.
3. Strain into a tall glass filled with fresh ice.
4. Top with soda water and garnish.
5. Raise your glass to the kite that *do not* get cut today.

Toasted Cumin Syrup Tip

Toast 1 tbsp cumin seeds till aromatic. Simmer with 1/2 cup jaggery (or sugar) and 1/2 cup water. Strain, cool, and store.

THE FINAL SIP

It's light. It's local. It fizzes with joy. Like Uttarayan itself—this drink was made to rise.

67

CHENNAI PONGAL PUNCH

The Rooftop Pongal Rebellion

The Story: Laughter, Liquor, and a Festival Twist

In Mylapore, Pongal doesn't just happen in kitchens.

It rises to rooftops—where cousins who haven't seen each other in a year gather to laugh louder than the temple drums and chase sunlight between clotheslines.

This year, Thatha's terrace was the battlefield.

The pongal was sweet and smoky, cooked in brass pots that had seen more festivals than most people in the family. Saffron swirled through the air, cardamom bloomed in every corner, and below, the rangoli faded quietly into the breeze.

Amid the warmth of jasmine and gossip, the older cousins—Nikhil, Meera, and Arvind—found what they'd always joked about but never touched:

Thatha's hidden stash.

A bottle of Indian single malt, aged longer than any of them had been legally allowed to drink.

They looked at each other.

'No one's going to know,' Nikhil whispered.

'It's a celebration,' Meera grinned.

'We're just...blending tradition,' said Arvind, already reaching for the ladle.

They poured just a finger of the whiskey.

Then, still warm from the pot, they added palm sugar syrup, lifted a pinch of fresh cardamom, and splashed in a few drops of lime.

It wasn't fancy. It wasn't stirred like the videos showed.

But when they took a sip, the rooftop breeze paused for a moment.

It tasted like sunshine.

Like sweetness after a fight. Like secrets that cousins never confess but always remember.

By the time the younger kids were herded downstairs and the elders were discussing turmeric prices, the 'Pongal Punch' had gone around the rooftop three rounds.

And Thatha? He knew. Of course he did.

Later that evening, as the sun dipped behind the temple gopuram, he sat beside Nikhil, took the glass from his hand, and took a slow sip.

He did not say a word. Just smiled.

And reached for the bottle.

What Makes This Cocktail Special?

Palm Sugar Syrup: Echoes the traditional Pongal pot with rich, smoky sweetness

Cardamom: Instantly festive, floral, and warming

Dry Ginger (*Sukku*): Adds authentic spice depth used in South Indian sweets

Whiskey: Bold and grounding, like an old family secret

Crafted on a Terrace, Not Behind a Bar: It's a toast to family, mischief, and moments you wish you could bottle

Ingredients
(Festive, Sweet, and Spiced)

- 60 ml Indian single malt or blended whiskey
- 20 ml palm sugar syrup
- 1 small pinch of ground cardamom
- 5 ml fresh lime juice
- 1 dash dry ginger powder (sukku)
- Ice cubes
- Garnish: A tiny jaggery shard or a twist of lime peel

How to Make It
(Festival Edition)

1. In a shaker or mixing glass, add the whiskey, palm sugar syrup, lime juice, and cardamom.
2. If using, add a tiny dash of sukku (dry ginger powder) for that Pongal pot authenticity.
3. Fill with ice and stir—don't shake—let the flavours blend like a rooftop conversation.
4. Strain into a rocks glass over fresh ice.
5. Garnish with a small jaggery piece on the rim or float a lime twist if feeling fancy.
6. Sip slowly, while remembering old cousins and new stories.

THE FINAL SIP

A festival in a glass—spiced, sun-warmed, and slightly rebellious.

This isn't just a drink.
It's a memory you did not plan to make.

68

BAISAKHI WHISKEY SMASH
Ganne Di Maar (Harvest Edition)

The Story: When Sugarcane Stole the Show

Every year on Baisakhi, the courtyard at Jasmeet's family farm near Patiala became a festival of its own. The *dhol* players never arrived on time, the *phulkas* were slightly burnt, and the generator failed by sunset—but no one cared.

It wasn't just about what went right.

It was about who showed up, what stories were retold, and which generation danced harder.

Jasmeet, the quiet one—the one who'd rather stir lassi than shout over music—had never been known for bold moves. But that year, as the sugarcane was cut and stacked beside the granary, an idea took root.

He remembered his nana, years ago, saying:

'Ganna is not just for chewing. It's the first thing we offer the land when it feeds us.'

That evening, while the aunties debated whether bhang was appropriate anymore, and the uncles had begun to repeat their old army tales, Jasmeet stood in the outer kitchen with a flask of fresh sugarcane juice, a bottle of Indian whiskey, and a pocketful of roasted fennel he had toasted earlier.

He crushed the fennel with his palm, added a squeeze of lime, a dash of kala namak, and poured in the sweet, greenish juice from the sugarcane.

Then came the whiskey. Just enough to warm the night without setting the fire.

No measurements. Just instinct and rhythm. He stirred it with the end of a sugarcane stick, took a sip—and paused.

The glass carried everything: The sweetness of the crop, the heat of the earth, the spice of memories, and the punch of mischief.

He handed the first glass to Uncle Ranjit, who raised an eyebrow and said, *'Hor koi tonic hai?'* Then took one sip, licked his lips, and called it: *'Ganne di maar.'*

The name stuck.

By the time the dhol players finally arrived, the kids were running sugarcane relay races, and Jasmeet's cocktail had been passed hand-to-hand like a whispered secret. It wasn't loud. It wasn't flashy.

But it was *perfect*. The kind of drink that doesn't come from a recipe—

It comes from the land, the people, and the moment they all exhale together under open sky.

Now, every Baisakhi, there's a line at Jasmeet's corner of the courtyard.

No one's asking for lassi anymore.

What Makes This Cocktail Special?

Fresh Sugarcane Juice: A direct sip from Punjab's harvest soul
Roasted Fennel Seeds: Adds warmth and familiar post-meal sweetness
Lime and Black Salt: Balances sweetness and adds complexity
Whiskey with Roots: Bold enough to carry the celebration
Light, Bright, and Ready to Dance: No heavy syrups, just farm-to-glass freshness

Ingredients
(Vibrant, Fresh, and Spiced)

- 60 ml Indian whiskey
- 15 ml fresh sugarcane juice
- 1/2 tsp roasted fennel seeds (crushed)
- 10 ml fresh lime juice
- A small pinch of black salt (kala namak)
- Ice cubes and garnish: Fennel-dusted lime wedge or a sugarcane stick if available

How to Make It
(With Harvest Hands)

1. Dry-roast fennel seeds, crush coarsely.
2. In a shaker, muddle fennel with sugarcane juice and lime juice.
3. Add whiskey and black salt, fill with ice.

4. Shake with rhythm (a bhangra beat is optional but recommended).
5. Strain into a rocks glass over fresh ice.
6. Garnish with a lime wedge dusted in fennel powder or a tiny sugarcane shard.

THE FINAL SIP

Harvest in a glass. Cooler than lassi.

Bolder than jaggery. And sharp enough to remind you:

Punjab doesn't just grow the grain—it knows how to raise a toast to it.

69

HOLI RANG MARTINI
When the Thandai Hit Different

The Story: The Year the Colours Glowed Back

Every Holi, it was Papa's job to bring the thandai.

Not because he was the best at it. But because he was the only one who still called the store manager 'beta' and got the good stuff—the kind made with hand-pounded almonds, poppy seeds, and nostalgia.

He had walked back home with two glass bottles clinking in a cloth bag, grinning through a cloud of pink gulaal, declaring, *'Ab party banegi!'*

Saurabh used to laugh at the drama. But this year, Papa was recovering from a cold, so Saurabh took the mission.

The Holi party prep was already chaos: cousins wrestling in the courtyard, aunties shouting over *gujiyas*, speakers testing which remix *of* 'Rang Barse' had the best bass. Saurabh ducked out, squeezed through the bazaar crowd, and found the thandai stall his father always swore by—tucked into the corner of the old market in Ujjain, just past the flower garland lane.

The vendor was ancient. Possibly eternal. Wearing a kurta so stained it looked like a Rangoli.

'One bottle, Holi special,' Saurabh said.

The man nodded slowly. He handed over a warm, slightly sloshed bottle with a glint in his eyes.

'Shivji ka prasad hai ye,' he said with reverence.

Saurabh, focused on party logistics, did not think twice. Prasad? Must be pure. Must be blessed.

Back home, he did what Papa always did. Mixed the thandai into the pre-chilled vodka. A little rose syrup. A twist of lime. A confident shake.

The first round went to the cousins. Then to the uncles.

Then to Tara, the neighbour who never usually stayed past snacks.

Everyone sipped. Then smiled. Then started hugging.

Thirty minutes in, Saurabh noticed something. Time had slowed. The colours were...brighter. Someone was dancing with the garden hose. Someone else was trying to feed a gujiya to the speaker.

And Papa?

He took one sniff of the drink and raised an eyebrow.

'Where'd you buy this thandai?' he asked, holding the glass like it was a relic.

'The same shop,' Saurabh said.

Papa took a slow sip. Smacked his lips.

Then smiled.

'Bhai...*woh wala prasad mil gaya tumhein*. The good stuff.'

It wasn't until hours later, when Tara and Saurabh were lying on the terrace, giggling at clouds, that he remembered the vendor's words.

Shivji ka prasad.

He closed his eyes, head spinning just the right amount. That martini? It wasn't just chilled.

It was cosmic.

What Makes This Cocktail Special?

Milk-washed Thandai Vodka: Clarified and silky, with traditional cooling spices like fennel, almonds, saffron, and cardamom

A Touch of Bhang: Optional, but essential to Holi's mischievous magic

Rose Syrup: For colour, floral depth, and celebration

Milk-washing Technique: Adds creamy elegance without actual dairy weight

Edible Petals: A finishing flourish that makes the drink as joyful as the festival itself

Ingredients
(Playful, Spiced, and Euphoric)

- 60 ml milk-washed vodka with thandai and bhang
- 15 ml rose syrup + 5 ml fresh lime juice
- Ice cubes
- Garnish: Dried edible petals (rose or marigold), silver varq optional—for colour, shine, and story

How to Make It
(Rang-Ready Ritual)

1. In a shaker, combine milk-washed vodka, rose syrup, and lime juice.
2. Fill with ice and shake briskly—imagine you are dodging water balloons while doing it.
3. Fine strain into a chilled coupe or martini glass.
4. Garnish with a sprinkle of dried petals. Float silver varq if you want extra dazzle.

5. Serve immediately, ideally with colour on your cheeks and music in the background.

Milk-Washed Vodka Prep Tip

- Warm 1 cup whole milk with 1 tbsp thandai mix and a pinch of bhang paste (optional).
- Let cool, then slowly stir into 250 ml vodka—don't rush, let it curdle.
- Rest for 1 hour, then strain through muslin or coffee filter until clear.
- Chill the clarified spirit in the fridge—it's the base magic of this cocktail.

THE FINAL SIP

A martini with mischief. Smooth as a lassi, pink as a rangoli, and laced with tradition, chaos, and a little divine sparkle.

This isn't just a drink—it's Holi in a glass.

70

KARVA CHAUTH MOONLIGHT MULE

Sip under the Stars

The Story: Rasam, Rest, and a Rooftop Toast

It was 10:03 p.m.

The moon had risen. The pooja was done. Plates were cleared. And Ananya had finally changed out of the lehenga that had tried to eat her ribs for twelve hours.

Her *saas*, Rekha, was already in the kitchen—unpinning her dupatta and humming an old film song while washing the steel thali. They hadn't spoken much all day. Not out of distance–just tradition. Too many guests. Too much vermicelli kheer. Too many *rules*.

Ananya was about to collapse onto the sofa when Rekha called out:

'Rooftop chalte hain?'

'No more rituals, please,' Ananya muttered. Rekha laughed. 'No rituals. Just a drink.'

Upstairs, the air was cool. Quiet. The kind of silence only rooftops in Indian cities know–one where the water tanks gossip and the wind remembers old stories.

Rekha pulled out a steel flask from a red bag. Two tumblers clinked against each other. She poured a pale, shimmery drink–delicate pink, with a floral scent and a hint of something sharp.

'Lychee, fennel, rose...aur thoda soda,' she said, handing over the glass. *'Main sugar fast karti hoon, not fun.'*

Ananya blinked. 'You made this?' Rekha winked. *'Rasam alag ho sakta hai. Par toast toh banta hai.'*

They clinked glasses. Took a sip. It was cold. Sweet but not clingy. Fragrant with something moonlit. They did not speak for a while.

Then Ananya sighed. 'You are not what I expected, you know.'

Rekha smiled. 'Neither are you.'

And just like that, under a moon they'd both fasted for in very different ways, something shifted. Not roles. Not status.

Just...comfort. And in a house full of rituals, that was the real celebration.

What Makes This Cocktail Special?

Fennel and Rose Syrup: A sweet, floral whisper of traditional flavours

Lychee Juice: Light and cooling, perfect for post-fast freshness
Edible Silver Dust: Optional shimmer, because you deserve a little glow

Ingredients
(Floral, Cooling and Silvery Sweet)

- 45 ml gin or white rum
- 30 ml lychee juice + 15 ml fennel and rose syrup
- 5 ml lime juice
- Ice cubes and soda water
- Garnish: A dash of edible silver dust, rose petal or lychee slice (optional)

How to Make It
(Moonrise Magic in a Glass)

1. In a shaker, combine gin or rum, lychee juice, fennel and rose syrup, and lime juice (if using).
2. Add ice and shake gently—no rush, no stress.
3. Strain into a highball or stemmed glass filled with fresh ice.
4. Top with soda and stir softly.
5. Garnish with silver dust, a petal, or simply your best smile.
6. Serve chilled, ideally after rituals, gossip, or forgiveness.

THE FINAL SIP

A drink for women who know fasting is only half the story.
Floral, fizzy, and just rebellious enough to sparkle.
This isn't just a cocktail. It's a rooftop truce with a twist.

MUMBAI MONSOON MANHATTAN
When the Rain Brings Someone Back

The Story: One Drink, Two Timelines, and Too Much Unsaid

It was supposed to be just another rainy Friday in Lower Parel.

An art show. Some blurry watercolours. A decent cheese platter. Nisha was about to leave when she saw him—standing alone near a painting of grey umbrellas and wire-hung saris.

Aarav.

Of course, it had to be now. In this weather. In this city that never forgot the exits people used.

They hadn't spoken in six years. Not since college. Not since that 3 a.m. phone call that ended with, 'Maybe it's just bad timing.'

But there he was—same slouch, same eyes. And a hesitant smile that hadn't aged.

They said hi. Awkwardly. Then a little more.

Then the rain started again—sharp, sudden, like Mumbai does. So they ducked into the nearest open bar, one of those barely-lit places with jazz on loop and menus written in chalk.

'I don't really drink,' she said, glancing at the smudged cocktail board.

'Same,' he said.

The bartender raised an eyebrow. 'Then tonight's the exception. Something slow. Strong. Storm-worthy.'

He stirred something amber with care. Poured it into two low glasses with a single cube of ice. Garnished it with a dried chilli that looked more symbolic than spicy.

'It's called the Mumbai Monsoon Manhattan,' he said. 'Smoky. Spicy. Like unresolved feelings.'

They laughed. Then sipped.

And something cracked open—not loud, not dramatic. Just warm. Real.

They did not talk about the past. Or what went wrong. Or what was still unsaid.

But as the thunder rolled and the ice clinked, Nisha looked at him and thought:

Maybe the city did not bring the wrong person back.

Maybe it just waited for the right rain.

What Makes This Cocktail Special?

Kokum-jaggery Reduction: A rich, coastal twist that replaces vermouth with something deeply local and seasonally tangy

Smoky Indian Single Malt: Bold and grounding, like wet pavement after the first thunderclap

Aromatic Bitters: Laced with clove and spice, evoking chai stalls and soaked mornings

Dried Red Chilli Garnish: A nod to the city's bite and the heat that lingers after the pour

Born in Mumbai, Stirred by its Skies: This isn't just a drink, it's a monsoon mood in a glass

Ingredients
(Moody, Spiced, and Spirit-Heavy)

- 50 ml Indian single malt
- 20 ml kokum-jaggery reduction
- 2 dashes aromatic bitters
- Ice cubes
- Garnish: Dried red chilli (for the heat) or a thin sliver of kokum rind (for drama)

How to Make Kokum-Jaggery Reduction

- Simmer 4-5 dried kokum peels with 1/3 cup crushed jaggery and 1/2 cup water.

- Add 1 crushed black pepper pod and a pinch of salt.
- Simmer for 8-10 minutes until slightly syrupy.
- Cool, strain, and store in fridge—good for 2-3 weeks.

How to Make It
(Stirred with Storm and Silence)

1. In a mixing glass, add single malt, kokum-jaggery reduction, and bitters.
2. Fill with ice and stir slowly—let the thunder roll.
3. Strain into a chilled lowball glass.
4. Garnish with a dried chilli or a sliver of kokum.
5. Sip while the city storms and old stories stir.

THE FINAL SIP

This isn't your grandfather's Manhattan.

It's monsoon in a glass—sharp, smoky, sweet, and just a little wild.

The kind of cocktail that doesn't ask questions.

It just brings you the answer...soaked in rain and memory.

72

HYDERABADI IRANI CHAI WHISKEY FLIP

A Sip for the Man behind the Counter

The Story: A Retiring Kettle, a Raising of Glasses

Aslam Bhai had poured over three lakh cups of chai. He did not count. But his customers did. Students, poets, rickshaw drivers, editors, lawyers, stage actors, and the occasional runaway groom—they all came to Café Safa for two things: the thick, sweet Irani chai that stuck to your soul, and the man who never forgot anyone's 'usual.'

For 45 years, he stood behind that curved marble counter like a lighthouse—metal saucers clinking, kettle hissing, steam rising like it had something to say. No clocks. No calculators. Just intuition, repetition, and rhythm.

Aslam Bhai had a rule: never rush the tea, never repeat the gossip, and always pour with the right hand.

And now, he was retiring.

The news spread faster than monsoon gossip. The café did not announce it—there was no poster, no discount, no fanfare. But by 7 p.m., every table was full. A few college kids came wearing t-shirts that said 'Chai Please, Bhai'. The old professor brought his chessboard. And in the corner, someone strummed a mandolin no one asked for.

Across the street, the tiny speakeasy bar—Peetal and Pepper—decided to do something special.

The bartender, Shyam, had grown up drinking Aslam Bhai's chai before tuition classes. He used to dunk Osmania biscuits and scribble love letters on the back of sugar packets. Now he mixed spirits instead of sugar. And tonight, he would mix a tribute.

Hyderabadi Irani Chai Whiskey Flip

He steeped Assam tea in cream, cracked in an egg yolk, added jaggery syrup, and shook it hard with Indian single malt. Then dusted it with saffron and a whisper of chai masala. The drink came out thick, glossy, and golden. The kind of drink that made you pause before the first sip.

He poured it into chilled steel tumblers—because 'Aslam Bhai would never serve anything in glass.'

'To Aslam Bhai,' Shyam said, raising his own drink. 'Chai that kicked like Scotch, and never spilled in a storm.'

People stood. Some with laughter. Some with tears.

Someone even brought out a plastic chair from Safa and placed it next to the bar, like the guest of honour needed an extra throne.

Aslam Bhai walked over slowly, dusted off the tumbler rim with his sleeve, and took a sip.

He paused. Let it settle. Then he smiled. 'It's not chai,' he said, adjusting his topi. 'But it's got heart.'

They all toasted again. Not to the drink—but to the man who poured with patience, stirred without spoons, and somehow, always knew when you needed a second cup before you asked.

What Makes This Cocktail Special?

Rich Assam Chai-infused Cream: A tribute to Hyderabad's thick Irani brews

Indian Single Malt: Adds strength and heritage with a slow-spice finish

Jaggery Syrup: Earthy sweetness that replaces sugar with memory

Egg Yolk: For that creamy, classic flip texture

Saffron and Chai masala Dust: A final flourish of café perfume and spice

Ingredients
(Creamy, Spiced, and Legacy-Laced)

- 50 ml Indian single malt + 25 ml jaggery syrup
- 30 ml strong Assam chai-infused cream
- 1 fresh egg yolk
- A pinch of chai masala
- A few strands of saffron
- Garnish: None. Or dust with masala for memory

How to Make It
(With Reverence and Rhythm)

1. In a shaker, combine whiskey, chai cream, jaggery syrup, egg yolk, chai masala, and saffron.
2. Dry shake first (no ice) to emulsify.
3. Add ice and shake again, hard, for 15-20 seconds.
4. Strain into a chilled steel tumbler or ceramic cup.
5. Serve with Osmania biscuits on the side, if you truly respect the legend.

THE FINAL SIP

This isn't just a flip. It's a farewell brewed with heart, spice, and quiet applause.

A drink for the man who never missed a pour. A memory you sip, not swallow.

73

SANDALWOOD AND SAFFRON GIN HIGHBALL

Wellness in a Tall Glass

The Story: The Drink after the Deep Tissue

The resort did not advertise the bar.

In fact, it wasn't even called a bar. It was tucked beside the meditation deck, past the bamboo arch and just beyond the silent lily pond. A hand-painted sign simply read: 'Sip and Settle.'

At 6:15 every evening—right when the sun slipped behind the Coorg treeline—guests began to appear, fresh from massages and hammams, hair damp, hearts slow.

There was no menu.

Just a copper urn, slices of Himalayan pink salt crystal on a tray, and a bartender named Karan who wore linen, not black.

'Something for the nerves,' someone would say. Or, 'Anything without guilt.' And always, from the regulars: 'The usual, please.'

The 'usual' was a sandalwood and saffron gin highball. Smooth. Aromatic. Almost silent on the tongue.

Karan steeped pure Mysore sandalwood chips in botanical gin for two days. Stirred in saffron syrup made in-house with just jaggery and patience. Topped it with mineral soda chilled in clay pots. And served it in tall glass tumblers with no garnish—just a single ice cube and a breath of quiet.

The first sip did not shout. It hummed.

Like temple bells from far away. Like the wind passing through frangipani.

Like the moment your thoughts stop talking back.

People came for the spa. But they stayed for this.

One guest, a tech CEO from Singapore, whispered after her third visit, 'This...this is the only part of the retreat I can't replicate.'

Karan just nodded.

Because some therapies come with hot stones.

Others come with sandalwood, saffron, and soda.

What Makes This Cocktail Special?

Sandalwood-infused Gin: Deeply calming, resinous, and subtly sacred

Saffron-jaggery Syrup: Soft floral notes balanced with earth-rich sweetness

Minimal Ice, No Garnish: Designed to be as meditative as it is mixological

Crafted like Therapy: Every element curated to relax and realign

Ingredients
(Aromatic, Calm, and Elegant)

- 45 ml sandalwood-infused gin
- 20 ml saffron-jaggery syrup
- Chilled soda water
- Ice–one large cube for slow chill
- Garnish: None. The aroma does the talking.

How to Make It
(Sip and Settle Style)

1. In a tall highball or ceramic glass, pour sandalwood gin and saffron syrup.
2. Add a large cube of ice. Stir gently–not rushed. Like you've just walked out of a sauna.
3. Top slowly with soda. Let the fizz settle itself.
4. Serve immediately, without a word. Let the scent do the welcome.

THE FINAL SIP

This isn't just a cocktail. It's stillness in a glass.

A botanical whisper that smells like memory and feels like calm.

The kind of drink that doesn't ask for company.

74

DECCAN SPICE NEGRONI

The Stubborn Spirit of the South

The Story: Dattanna's Glass, Dattanna's Rules

At 80, Dattanna still drank.

Not recklessly. Not socially. Just one drink. Every evening. Same glass. Same chair. Same judgemental look at anyone who dared suggest a light beer.

It wasn't about the alcohol. It was about the ritual.

His drink of choice? A Negroni—well, sort of. He had tweaked it decades ago, replacing foreign bitters with dried kokum from the backyard tree and infusing the gin with cinnamon bark his late wife used to drop into her Sunday biryani.

The family called it stubborn. He called it heritage.

'It keeps me from turning British on the inside,' He had grumble, swirling the crimson concoction in a glass older than most of his grandchildren.

Every year, they tried to change him.

'Appa, try this new low-ABV spritz.' 'No, Thaatha, we got you this fancy Japanese whiskey.'

'This year, no drinking—Doctor's orders!'

And every year, He had nod politely, listen patiently, and at exactly 6:45 p.m., pour himself a Deccan Spice Negroni.

One part gin, one part kokum-syrup vermouth, one part bitter liqueur he had refused to name.

He stirred it without fuss, no shaker, no garnish. Just a sliver of dried kokum sunk to the bottom like a secret he wasn't ready to tell.

At Diwali gatherings, someone always tried to impress him with a 'smoked margarita' or 'desi Old-Fashioned'.

He had to take a sip, wince, and mutter:

'Yeh sab drama hai. Real drink toh bite karta hai.'

And that's what the Deccan Spice Negroni was—sharp, complex, earthy. Like its maker.

When he passed, they found a notebook under his cot. Four pages were blank. The fifth held only one thing:

1. Take what's foreign.
2. Add what's yours.
3. Stir with pride.

Now, every year, on his birthday, the family makes a batch. Some still wince at the kokum. But they drink it anyway.

Because no matter what they believe in—

Everyone agrees: Dattanna was right about the gin.

What Makes This Cocktail Special?

Dried Kokum: A bold, tangy twist that replaces citrus and bitters with Deccan soul

Cinnamon-infused Gin: Warm, spicy, and just nostalgic enough to taste like memory

Indian Sweet Vermouth: Blended with kokum syrup or tamarind hint

Unapologetically Red: A hue as bold as Dattanna's opinions

Stirred, Never Shaken: Because that's how rebels roll

Ingredients
(Bold, Spiced, and Heritage-Laced)

- 30 ml cinnamon-infused gin
- 30 ml kokum-spiced sweet vermouth
- 30 ml Campari (or Indian bitter liqueur)
- Ice—cubed, no crushed nonsense
- Garnish: Dried kokum slice or cinnamon stick

How to Make It
(Old School, Always)

1. In a mixing glass, combine gin, vermouth, and bitters.
2. Add ice and stir gently—no rush, no show.
3. Strain into a rocks glass over one big cube.
4. Drop a dried kokum slice in the bottom. Let it rest like Dattanna's wisdom.
5. Sip slow. Argue faster.

THE FINAL SIP

This isn't your mixologist's Negroni.

It's fire and bark, fruit and fight.

A cocktail that doesn't care for fads—only roots.

One sip, and you'll understand why some men never change.

Kanyakumari Old-Fashioned

75

KANYAKUMARI OLD-FASHIONED
A Measure of Salt, Time, and Memory

The Story: The Lighthouse Still Knows

No one remembers when Bala Master stopped keeping time for the lighthouse.

Only that he still showed up every evening.

The sea had retired him. Or maybe bureaucracy did. But the routine remained: just before the first beam blinked across the Kanyakumari sky, he settled into the same granite bench overlooking the water—salt-bitten, worn, steady.

And he poured himself a drink.

It wasn't fancy. Just the same three things, every time:

Whiskey. A few drops of his homemade banana flower bitters. A spoon-tip of crushed spice blend he ground fresh every week.

And—always—a pinch of sea salt scraped from the edges of dried shells, sun-cured by his own hand.

He stirred it in a clay cup. No garnish. No ice. Just warmth and intention.

When the young tourists asked why he still did it—this ceremony of one—he shrugged and said, 'Because the sea still keeps time. And so do I.'

Some days, he had to say more.

'That banana flower? My wife's favourite curry.

'That spice mix? My mother's sambhar *podi* without the turmeric.

'That salt? That's from the day my son was born. We dried it on the terrace.'

To most, the drink was strong. Too strong.

To Bala Master, it was exact. A language without vowels.

A ritual where silence was seasoning.

The lighthouse blinked. The sea answered.
And so did he—with one long sip.
Not to forget.
But to remember exactly.

What Makes This Cocktail Special?

Banana Flower Bitters: Earthy, floral bitterness rooted in regional flavour
Hand-ground Coastal Spice: Typically with black pepper, fennel, dried ginger
Sea Salt: Not just seasoning—emotion

Ingredients
(Earthy, Coastal, and Quietly Bold)

- 60 ml Indian whiskey or smoky bourbon
- 2 dashes banana flower bitters + 1/4 tsp coastal spice blend
- A pinch of sea salt
- Ice cube (optional, one large)
- Garnish: None. Drink doesn't need it

How to Make It
(The Lighthouse Ritual)

1. In a mixing glass or clay cup, combine whiskey, bitters, spice blend, and sea salt.
2. Stir gently—no rush. Let the salt dissolve with memory.
3. Strain into a heavy-bottomed rocks glass (or keep in clay, traditional style).
4. Add one cube of ice, or none, as per your own rhythm.
5. Sip slow. Listen for the sea.

THE FINAL SIP

This isn't just an Old-Fashioned.

It's Kanyakumari's pulse in a pour—salty, grounded, and a little stubborn.

A drink made not for company, but for continuity.

The kind of cocktail that doesn't chase time. It keeps it.

76

PUMPKIN PEEL WHISKEY SOUR

From Scrap to Spirit

The Story: Nani's Rule, Reimagined in Guwahati

Dia still remembered the exact tone her Nani used.

Not scolding. Not sweet. Just certain.

'If it smells good, it still has work to do.'

It applied to mango peels, coriander stems, and especially pumpkin skins—which her grandmother would sun-dry, grind into sabzi masala, or pickle with mustard and love.

Now, years later, Dia stood behind the bar at a rooftop café in Guwahati, far from her Nani's kitchen, but never far from her rules.

It was Halloween season, and the place was overflowing with carved pumpkin décor—smiling faces, twisted stems, and mounds of wasted skin.

One afternoon, Dia saw a staff member dumping a tray of pumpkin peels near the compost bin.

She stopped him.

'Wait. Let me try something.'

She charred the peels on a cast iron pan, steeped them in jaggery water with a pinch of black salt and toasted cumin. The result smelled...familiar. Like her grandmother's winter pantry and the dusky corners of the old spice cupboard.

She stirred the syrup into a whiskey sour base—local grain whiskey, lemon, a bit of tamarind for tang—and gave it a dry shake with aquafaba.

It poured golden, cloud-soft, and smoky. On the first sip, it was comfort. On the second, it was clever. On the third, it was a memory.

Now, every time she made it, she heard Nani's voice in the back of her head:

'Good. You listened.'

What Makes This Cocktail Special?

Charred Pumpkin Peel Syrup: Earthy, smoky, and unexpectedly sweet

Local Indian Whiskey: Bold, grain-forward, a canvas for spice

Jaggery + Tamarind: For balanced sweetness and a tangy layer

Black Salt and Toasted Cumin: For that savoury edge and ancestral soul

A Cocktail Born from 'Waste': And worth every saved peel

Ingredients
(Rooted, Warm, and Waste-Free)

- 50 ml Indian grain whiskey
- 25 ml pumpkin peel syrup
- 15 ml fresh lemon juice
- 10 ml tamarind water—optional, for tang
- 20 ml aquafaba (or egg white)—for foam
- Garnish: Dehydrated pumpkin crisp or lime peel twist

How to Make It
(The Nani Way)

1. Make the syrup: Roast pumpkin peels till smoky. Simmer in jaggery water with black salt and toasted cumin. Strain and cool.
2. In a shaker, combine all ingredients except garnish.
3. Dry shake (no ice) to build froth.
4. Add ice and shake again until well chilled.
5. Strain into a coupe or rocks glass.
6. Garnish with a pumpkin crisp or nothing at all—Nani would not need decoration.

THE FINAL SIP

This isn't just a whiskey sour. It's a second life.

A saved skin. And a grandmother's voice that turned 'leftovers' into legacy.

77

OVERRIPE PAPAYA DAIQUIRI

The Papaya Redemption in Vizag

The Story: The Roommate, the Rotting Fruit, and the Unexpected Party

Rhea knew something was off the moment she opened the door.

Not the music. Not the open sandals by the shoe rack. Not even the faint scent of coconut hair oil from next door.

It was...the papaya.

A massive one, half-slouched on the kitchen counter like it had given up on life. Her roommate Anjali had bought it three days ago–full of good intentions and zero chopping motivation.

Now it was bruised, soft, and collapsing in on itself.

Rhea was about to bin it, but paused. They had white rum. Some limes. Jaggery syrup. And in the pantry, a sprinkle tin from Anjali's mom labelled *'Vizag Gongura Salt - Extra Khara!'*

Five minutes later, the blender was roaring.

She scooped the papaya flesh, squeezed in lime, added the jaggery, threw in a few cubes of ice and a double pour of rum. She shook it with casual flair, strained it into two salt-rimmed glasses, and dusted a *tiny* pinch of gongura salt over the foam.

Anjali took one sip and blinked. 'That tastes like... revenge and vacation.'

By 8 p.m., the flat had a crowd.

Someone brought peanuts. Someone played an old Illayaraja mix. The blender whirred through at least four more batches.

And when someone asked what this drink was called, Rhea shrugged.

'Papaya Redemption.'

Because in Vizag, even your roommate's rotten fruit deserves a second chance.

What Makes This Cocktail Special?

Overripe Papaya: Too soft to slice, just right to blend
Jaggery Syrup: Earthy sweetness, home-style and balanced
Gongura Salt: Andhra's tangy-spicy-salty magic in a microdose
White Rum: Clean, tropical base that loves fruit
Blender over Shaker: Because this isn't fine dining–it's flat-party flair

Ingredients
(Tangy, Tropical, and Totally Redeemed)

- 50 ml white rum
- 70 g overripe papaya flesh
- 20 ml fresh lime juice
- 15 ml jaggery syrup—1:1 jaggery to water, simmered and cooled
- Pinch of gongura salt—optional
- Ice cubes
- Garnish: Gongura salt rim or just a lime wedge

How to Make It
(Flatmate-Approved Method)

1. Blend papaya, lime juice, jaggery syrup, rum, and ice until smooth.
2. Optional: Rim a chilled glass with lime and dip in gongura salt.
3. Strain or pour directly into a chilled glass (rocks or coupe).
4. Sprinkle a touch of gongura salt on top for a savoury kick.
5. Serve immediately. And then make another batch.

THE FINAL SIP

This isn't just about saving fruit.
It's about saving the evening.
A daiquiri that forgives, forgets, and finishes with a smile.
Papaya never had it this good.

78

TAMARIND PEEL VODKA COOLER

Sacred Sour, Spirited Smooth

The Story: Shade, Scrap, and a Sip That Stuck

Some call Puri a temple town.

For Neel, it was a flavour town.

He was a bartender from Bhubaneshwar, down for a short stint—part coastal escape, part sabbatical, part palate cleanse. While most tourists came for the rituals, Neel roamed the side lanes for smells. Ghee. Banana leaf steam. Tamarind heat hanging in the air like prayer flags.

One morning, walking past a massive temple kitchen, he noticed something odd.

Mounds of tamarind peels—deep brown, curled like wood shavings—being shovelled off into bags after massive *dal* preparations. The fragrance stopped him. He stared. Then stepped forward.

'Ye sab fek dete ho?'

'Peel hai, bhai. Kaam ka nahi,' the worker shrugged.

Neel nodded, smiled politely, and walked off.

Then circled back five minutes later with an empty jute sack.

Back in Bhubaneshwar, he roasted the peels till smoky. Boiled them gently with jaggery and a little black salt. The result was a syrup that smelled like shade under a banyan tree. Tart, rich, earthy—and humming with something that felt old.

He added it to a simple vodka cooler—lime, soda, ice.

And paused. It wasn't holy. But it was close.

It had the tang of temple thalis, the comfort of afternoon naps, and the clarity of rituals repeated for centuries.

He put it on the specials board: Tamarind Peel Vodka Cooler.

When someone asked what it was, he simply said:

'From the scraps of something sacred.'

What Makes This Cocktail Special?

Tamarind Peel: Waste no more; roasted and reborn into earthy tang (made from roasted tamarind peel, jaggery, black salt)
Jaggery: Brings warmth and soul to the syrup
Black Salt: Adds minerality and a savory hum
Vodka: A neutral base that lets the peel shine
Soda and Lime: To lift, stretch, and cool the drink like monsoon breeze in temple shade

Ingredients
(Sacred, Scrappy, and Summer-Ready)

- 45 ml vodka
- 25 ml tamarind peel syrup + 15 ml fresh lime juice
- Chilled soda water
- Ice–cubed
- Garnish: Dried tamarind peel ribbon or lime wheel

How to Make It
(Blessed and Stirred)

1. Make the syrup**:** Roast dried tamarind peels. Simmer with equal parts jaggery and water. Add a pinch of black salt. Cool and strain.
2. In a shaker, combine vodka, tamarind peel syrup, and lime juice.
3. Shake with ice and strain into a tall glass filled with fresh ice.
4. Top with chilled soda. Stir gently.
5. Garnish subtly. This drink speaks quietly.

THE FINAL SIP

This isn't fusion. It's faith, filtered through a cooler.

A cocktail made from what others discard.

A drink that tastes like rituals reimagined—and summer rescued.

79

CARROT-ORANGE HIGHBALL
The Legend of Room 42

The Story: MBA, Masala, and the Mixer That Made Them Famous

Room 42 of the Old SIC Boys Hostel at Symbiosis, Hinjewadi, wasn't famous for grades.

They had one guy barely making it through macroeconomics, another rewatching *Shark Tank* to 'feel productive,' and a half-dead money plant named 'HR Policy.'

But in their final semester, just before placement season panic hit full steam, they became legendary—for a drink.

It started with Yogesh.

Yogesh wasn't the topper of the batch. But he was on the Mess Committee—and that meant he had *access*. Ice when the freezer was locked. Extra oranges when no one else got fruit. And the kind of mysterious power that ensured *chakna* appeared even when the budget did not. If you wanted something from the mess, you called Yogesh. And if you gave him enough time and a juicer, he had probably hand you a cocktail, too.

One Sunday, post a brutally boring lecture on consumer

behaviour and a failed group PPT, the boys returned to find Yogesh in the kitchen surrounded by carrot pulp.

'What happened to the juice?' someone asked.

'Finished. This is the good part,' he grinned.

Using leftover carrot pulp, some squashed oranges from the mess fruit basket, soda, and the vodka they'd been hoarding in an old casebook titled *Strategic Financial Analysis*, Yogesh stirred up a drink. For balance, he added a bit of black salt, chilli powder, and just a whiff of grated ginger.

He called it 'Carrot-Orange Highball—Version Hostel.'

It fizzed like ambition and tasted like a 6.5 CGPA with startup dreams.

By 8:30 p.m., the drink had been batch-made in a pressure cooker vessel, served in paper cups with cracked ice from a hostel ice tray. The corridor started filling up—people from Rooms 17 to 51. Even that one guy who never left his room unless there was biryani.

And suddenly, Room 42 had purpose.

'Drink this,' Yogesh said. 'It's got vitamins *and* vodka.'

By the time placement season rolled around, no one remembered their last case study. But they all remembered the drink that made them forget it.

What Makes This Cocktail Special?

Carrot Pulp: Saved from waste, rich in colour, body, and nostalgia

Orange Juice: Fresh, messy, whatever was left in the mess crate

Ginger and Chilli: For zing, heat, and that 'hostel edge'

Black Salt: To add complexity (and probably mask the vodka brand)

Soda: For sparkle and hydration between job rejections

Vodka: Because whiskey was too expensive

Ingredients
(Zesty, Waste-Smart, and MBA-Approved)

- 50 ml vodka
- 30 ml orange juice
- 20 ml carrot pulp syrup
- 10 ml lime juice
- Chilled soda water
- Ice—cracked from a hostel fridge
- Garnish: Orange zest twist (if someone's feeling fancy)

How to Make It
(The Hostel Way)

1. Make the syrup: Simmer carrot pulp with sugar, black salt, a chilli pinch, and crushed ginger. Strain and cool.
2. In a jug or large glass, mix vodka, syrup, orange juice, and lime.
3. Add ice. Stir with a hostel spoon or steel straw.
4. Top with soda. Stir once more.
5. Serve in paper cups. Accept applause.

THE FINAL SIP

This isn't just a highball.

It's jugaad in a glass.

A cocktail born from leftovers, deadlines, and desperation.

The drink that made Room 42 unforgettable.

Even if their final grades weren't.

80

GUAVA SEED GIN SPRITZ

From Hampi, with a Hint of Heat

The Story: Market Mischief, Seed Secrets, and the Spritz That Travelled the World

Hampi had a vibe.

Not just the ruins, the boulders, or the temples that seemed carved by time itself—but the rhythm of chai carts, rooftop cafés, and a backpacker energy that hummed like tabla beats under moonlight.

Zoya had moved here for a month. It had been six.

She ran the bar at a boutique hostel café that served turmeric risotto, jackfruit tacos, and playlists that switched from Kishore Kumar to Bonobo without warning.

Every Saturday, she strolled through the local farmers' market with a backpack and no shopping list—just instinct.

That's when she saw him.

The fruit vendor. Dimpled grin, rolled sleeves, surrounded by crates of guavas.

He was slicing, straining, and discarding the seeds like they meant nothing.

She paused. 'What do you do with those?'

'These? *Kachra*,' he laughed, wiping his hands on his lungi.

'Mind if I take some home?' she asked.

He grinned again. 'You are not gonna plant guava trees in that bag, are you?'

Back in her bar, Zoya washed the seeds, sun-dried them, and toasted them gently with black pepper and coriander. She dropped them into gin and let it sit for two days.

The infusion came out fragrant—tangy with a sneaky heat, like flirtation with a punchline.

She built a spritz with lime, sugar, soda, and the guava-seed gin. Pale pink. Slightly fizzy. Unapologetically playful.

The first tourist who tried it ordered two.

The second asked if it could be bottled.

By week's end, a London travel vlogger called it 'the best cocktail in India, full stop.'

Zoya named it the Guava Seed Gin Spritz.

And every Saturday, she still walked past the vendor, who now saved the seeds in a separate basket, waiting for her with a smile and a wink.

What Makes This Cocktail Special?

Guava Seed-infused Gin: Subtle heat and tropical tang from what's usually trashed
Fresh Lime: Adds brightness and balance
Coriander and Pepper: For earthy, floral spice
Simple Syrup: Just enough to round it out
Soda Water: To lift and lighten
Made in Hampi: Enjoyed around the world

Ingredients
(Playful, Tangy, and Travel-Ready)

- 45 ml guava seed-infused gin (seeds toasted with black pepper and coriander, steeped for 48 hours)
- 15 ml lime juice
- 15 ml simple syrup
- Chilled soda water
- Ice–cubed
- Garnish: Guava slice or dried seed rim

How to Make It
(Backpacker Bar Edition)

1. In a shaker, mix infused gin, lime juice, and syrup.
2. Shake with ice briefly–just enough to mix.

3. Strain into a highball or wine glass over ice.
4. Top with soda and stir gently.
5. Garnish with a thin slice of guava—or a rim of crushed guava seeds if you are showing off.

THE FINAL SIP

This isn't your average spritz.

It's a cocktail born from discarded seeds, sun-scorched stone markets, and one really good grin.

A drink that made Hampi taste like summer.

And made the world ask,

'Why haven't we tried this before?'

81

GULAB JAMUN RUM FLOAT
Sweet Sin in a Crystal Glass

The Story: Legacy, Liquor, and a Little Floating Rebellion

The shop had been there for 86 years.

Tucked into a narrow street in North Kolkata, just a few lanes down from College Street, it did not need signage. The smell of hot syrup and cardamom was its own GPS.

'Mukherjee Mishtir Dokaan' was famous for two things: its saffron-drenched gulab jamuns and its unwavering refusal to modernize.

That is—until Arindam came home.

Fresh from a mixology course in Singapore and bearing a very un-Bengali tattoo of a jigger on his wrist, Arindam was the third-generation heir to the shop. But unlike his father and grandfather, he saw sugar not as tradition—but as potential.

One night, after helping close the shop, Arindam stayed behind.

The kitchen was quiet. The brass syrup pot still warm. He took a ladle of the rose-cardamom syrup, added a pinch of clove and cinnamon bitters, and poured it over a base of dark, oak-aged Indian rum. Then—because he could not help himself—he floated a single mini gulab jamun in the glass.

It looked ridiculous. It looked rebellious.

It looked perfect.

As he reached for a bar spoon, the old wood door creaked open.

His father stood there. In kurta, yawning.

They made eye contact. Silence.

Then, Arindam handed him the glass.

His father took a long sip. Let it sit.

Then smacked his lips, looked at the jamun bobbing like a moon in molasses, and said:

'Not bad, beta. Just...don't serve it to Dadu.'

Arindam laughed. He knew his grandfather would call it sacrilege. Or worse—'fusion'.

But as his father reached for a second glass, he added with a wink:

'Relax, Baba. I'll serve Dadu the sugar-free one.'

His father chuckled—because everyone knew Dadu hated sugar-free anything.

But for the first time, between the syrup, the spice, and the slow warmth of the rum—

Arindam's mishti cocktail did not feel like rebellion.

It felt like *inheritance—just stirred differently.*

What Makes This Cocktail Special?

Mini Gulab Jamun: Not garnish. Centrepiece.
Indian Dark Rum: Bold, oak-aged, and caramel-kissed
Rose-cardamom Syrup: Sweet nostalgia, spiced with heritage
Clove and Cinnamon Bitters: Adds depth and a whisper of heat
Syrup from Mishti Traditions: Elevated, not erased

Ingredients
(Bold, Sweet, and Bengali-Boozy)

- 45 ml Indian dark rum
- 20 ml rose-cardamom syrup
- 2 dashes clove and cinnamon bitters
- 1 mini gulab jamun
- Ice—one large cube
- Garnish: None. Let the jamun float like a moon

How to Make It
(Late-Night Legacy Version)

1. In a mixing glass, stir together the rum, rose syrup, and bitters with a large ice cube.
2. Strain into a lowball or coupe glass.
3. Gently float a mini gulab jamun on top.
4. Don't overdo the garnish. This drink already has a story.
5. Sip slowly. Let the syrup melt the line between tradition and twist.

THE FINAL SIP

This isn't dessert. It's disruption.

A mishti turned mixology.

A cocktail that says: You can honour tradition—

Even as you pour something new over it.

82

JALEBI WHISKEY FLIP

Sweet Cream, Spiced Heat, Hotel Secrets

The Story: After Hours, after Sugar, after Rules

It started with tired feet.

Every night at the Grand Calypso Hotel in Bangalore, just past 1:00 a.m., the pastry chef Meher would plop down at the back counter of the bar—sugar-smudged chef coat, hairnet still clinging on, and always with a plate of 'unsellable' jalebis.

Spirals too flat, syrup too thin, edges too burnt—hotel rejects.

Her rule? If she could not plate it, she had to drink it.

So she dunked a jalebi in whatever the bartender, Vikram, was experimenting with that night. Bourbon, Scotch, an expired Baileys bottle once.

One Thursday, she brought condensed milk. 'For rasmalai base,' she claimed.

Vikram smirked. 'Let's put it to better use.'

He cracked an egg. Added whiskey. Poured in a shot of condensed milk. A thread of saffron. Shook the mix until the tin was ice-cold.

Then dropped in half a jalebi—just for drama.

They tasted. And paused.

It was ridiculous. It was perfect. It was *rasmalai*, rum, and rebellion in a coupe glass. They called it their Jalebi Whiskey Flip—sweet, rich, unapologetic.

Every night, after service, they made one. No recipe. Just instinct.

Until one evening, the GM walked in early for his espresso. Took a sip from Meher's glass. Raised an eyebrow.

'Put it on the VIP list,' he said. 'And tell the mixologist to wear gloves.'

Meher winked at Vikram. Vikram just poured another round.

And from that night on, every glass that left the kitchen whispered one thing:

'The chefs drink better than the guests.'

What Makes This Cocktail Special?

Jalebi Syrup: Caramelized, floral, and sticky-sweet chaos
Condensed Milk: Velvety texture and nostalgia in a pour
Egg Yolk: For that classic flip thickness
Saffron: Because it would not be five-star without it

Ingredients
(Decadent, Silky, and Mischievously Desi)

- 45 ml Indian whiskey
- 20 ml condensed milk + 15 ml jalebi syrup
- 1 egg yolk
- A few threads of saffron
- Garnish: Half a jalebi spiral or a fine grating of nutmeg

How to Make It
(Pastry Kitchen After-Hours Style)

1. In a shaker, combine whiskey, condensed milk, jalebi syrup, egg yolk, and saffron.
2. Dry shake (no ice)—hard to emulsify.
3. Add ice and shake again until the tin feels like marble.
4. Strain into a chilled coupe or stemmed glass.
5. Garnish with a floating mini jalebi, or a fine saffron thread swirl.

THE FINAL SIP

This isn't your standard flip. It's the dessert tray's rebellion.

A cocktail whipped up when the lights go low and the chefs start playing.

One drink—and you'll know why the real magic at five-stars happens after the guests leave.

83

KESARI BADAM RUM PUNCH

Jokes, Nerves, and One Spiked Memory

The Story: Mom's Milk, Dad's Secret, and the Drink That Landed Every Punchline

Ravi did not believe in luck. He believed in rituals.

He had tried all of them—left sock first, no green room selfies, chewing tulsi before mic check. But the one that stuck? A sip of *something warm, nutty, and slightly illegal* before stepping onstage.

It started years ago, in the balcony of his family's flat in Andheri East.

When he was a kid, his mom would bring him a warm glass of kesar badam doodh before every school recitation. 'For the brain,' she said.

Later, as a teenager, he discovered that his dad kept a bottle of dark rum behind the tin of rajma.

And somewhere between stage fright and failed open mics, those two memories fused.

Now in his late 20s and hosting Thursday nights at a suburban comedy club, Ravi had a new superstition: no show without his almond-saffron pre-set sip.

One night, after bombing a set, he slumped at the bar and told his friend Sam—the in-house bartender—about his odd pre-show mix.

Sam raised an eyebrow. 'Badam doodh...with rum?'

Ravi nodded. 'Don't knock it till your punchlines land.'

An hour later, Sam brought over a glass. It shimmered golden. Smelled like Diwali and rebellion.

'I blended almond cream, saffron syrup, and your usual dark rum,' he said. 'With a squeeze of lime. Just to keep it...awake.'

Ravi took a sip.

It was warm, bold, nostalgic. Like a childhood bedtime story laced with just enough chaos to keep it interesting.

That night, his set landed. Every joke. Every callback. Even the pun about Zoom fatigue got a round of applause.

From then on, he had a new ritual. He called it Kesari Punchline.

Sam just called it profit.

What Makes This Cocktail Special?

Badam (Almond) Cream: Nutty base, creamy and rich
Saffron Syrup: Aromatic luxury with a golden hue

Dark Rum: Comfort, confidence, and slight mischief
Fresh Lime Juice: To slice through the sweetness

Ingredients
(Comforting, Confident, and Slightly Illicit)

- 45 ml Indian dark rum
- 30 ml almond milk or cream + 20 ml saffron syrup
- 10 ml lime juice
- Ice–cubed
- Garnish: Toasted almond flakes or a tiny pinch of saffron on top

How to Make It
(Pre-Show Ritual Approved)

1. In a shaker, add all ingredients except garnish.
2. Shake hard with ice to chill and emulsify.
3. Strain into a chilled coupe or rocks glass over a big cube.
4. Garnish with a few toasted almond slivers or a whisper of saffron.

THE FINAL SIP

This isn't just a rum punch. It's a back-of-the-mind memory stirred with late-night confidence. A drink for the dreamers, the jokers, the misfits with a mic.

And the perfect reminder that the best punchlines... need just a little punch.

84

SOAN PAPDI SMASH

Flaky Sweet, Fiercely Shaken

The Story: A Bartender, a Grudge, and a Mithai Redemption Arc

Pooja had two rules.

One—never serve a cocktail she would not drink herself.

Two—never touch Soan Papdi. Not to eat. Not to gift. And definitely not to forgive.

As a pastry-chef-turned-bartender in Mumbai's most meme-worthy microbrew bar, Pooja had fought for flavour. For texture. For respect.

And then came Diwali.

By day three, the back counter of the bar was drowning in re-gifted boxes of Soan Papdi. Some still in the same wrappers. One with three name tags layered like failed Tinder bios.

'I swear this sweet has more air than identity,' she muttered.

But instead of rage-quitting, she did what legends do—she fought fire with flavour.

Pooja crushed the flaky, sugar-stranded cubes into powder. Toasted them gently with citrus peel for depth. Then rimmed a coupe glass like it was the edge of a throne.

In the shaker: Aromatic gin. Fresh lemon.

Saffron syrup she had leftover from an attempted mithai shooter experiment.

A single basil leaf, just to say she was still fancy. She shook it hard, poured it bright, and let the rim glitter.

The Soan Papdi Smash.

The first guest took a sip. Eyebrows lifted.

The second asked if he could Instagram the garnish.

The third said, 'Wait—this is...actually Soan Papdi?'

And just like that, the protest became a podium. Pooja did not say 'I told you so.' She just made another round.

What Makes This Cocktail Special?

Crushed Soan Papdi Rim: Flaky, caramelized, sarcastic perfection
Saffron Syrup: Rich, floral, Diwali-in-a-pour
Lemon Juice: Sharp and bright, like Pooja's comebacks
Aromatic Gin: Light, spiced, a clean contrast to all that nostalgia

Ingredients
(Bold, Zesty, and Rim-Rescuing)

- 50 ml aromatic Indian gin
- 20 ml lemon juice + 20 ml saffron syrup
- 1 basil leaf—torn
- Crushed Soan Papdi
- Ice
- Garnish: Soan Papdi rim + saffron thread or lemon twist

How to Make It
(From Hate Gift to Hero Glass)

1. Crush Soan Papdi into a flaky powder and toast lightly with citrus zest.
2. Rim a rocks glass with lemon juice and dip into the papdi crumble.
3. In a shaker, combine gin, lemon juice, saffron syrup, and basil (if using).
4. Add ice. Shake till frosty and then strain into the rimmed glass. Garnish as dramatically as you wish.
5. Sip with mischief. Serve with shade.

THE FINAL SIP

This isn't a cocktail. It's revenge. A flaky re-gift turned golden redemption.

And proof that even the most mocked mithai...can make a damn fine drink.

85

MYSORE PAK OLD-FASHIONED
Rent Relief, Brown Butter, and Bengaluru Charm

The Story: One Sip, No Hike

Malleswaram is known for many things—Raghavendra stores, crisp dosas, slow mornings.

And now, one cocktail.

Arjun lived on the second floor of an old apartment block, above a retired RBI officer named Subramaniam Uncle—who believed two things:

1. Rent should rise annually, like inflation.
2. Alcohol was for 'those Bombay types.'

When the 'modest hike' notice arrived—8% this year, plus maintenance—Arjun decided to act fast.

No long emails. No society meetings.

Just...a drink.

Arjun worked at a culinary co-working space and had recently learned how to fat-wash whiskey using brown butter.

He steeped it slowly—rich, nutty, and golden. Stirred in jaggery syrup with a tiny pinch of flaky salt. And for flair, placed a cube of Mysore Pak right on the rim.

He knocked on Uncle's door just before his evening Suprabhatam playlist started.

'Uncle, try this,' he said. 'Made it myself. No pressure.'

The old man looked at the glass like it was suspiciously modern art. Took a whiff. Raised one eyebrow.

One sip. Pause. Smack of lips.

'Hm. Cheeky bugger.'

He did not say yes. But the next morning, a fresh notice was slipped under Arjun's door.

'Rent unchanged. But next time—make two.'

What Makes This Cocktail Special?

Brown Butter-fat-washed Whiskey: Rich, velvety, and deep
Jaggery Syrup: Earthy sweetness that ties it to the South
Flaky Sea Salt: For contrast and complexity

Mysore Pak: Not a garnish. A statement.

Ingredients
(Earthy, Elegant, and Slightly Strategic)

- 50 ml brown butter: fat-washed bourbon or Indian whiskey
- 10 ml jaggery syrup
- 1-2 dashes aromatic bitters or clove/cardamom bitters
- Pinch of flaky salt
- Garnish: A mini square of Mysore Pak on the rim
- Ice—one big cube

How to Make It
(Landlord-Level Smooth)

1. Fat-wash the whiskey: Melt ghee or brown unsalted butter, mix with whiskey, freeze overnight, strain the next day.

2. In a mixing glass, stir the fat-washed whiskey, jaggery syrup, bitters, and salt with ice.
3. Strain into a chilled rocks glass over a large cube.
4. Gently place a mini Mysore Pak on the rim or alongside.
5. Serve warm, with a smile—and your rent agreement ready.

THE FINAL SIP

This isn't just a drink. It's rent control, caramelized.

A sweet, spiced reminder that sometimes...hospitality outranks haggling.

The Maharaja's Cipher

86

THE MAHARAJA'S CIPHER

A Scroll Wrapped in Silk

The Story: A Secret Steeped in Shadows

London, 2024.

Lot #1897 passed almost unnoticed—a worn scroll, bound in maroon silk, misfiled under 'culinary miscellany.'

But beneath that faded seal lay something no auctioneer could decipher.

A royal cipher.

Penned in the precise, slanted script of a Tikamgarh heir, the manuscript held more than ink—it held a ritual. A potion passed from sovereign to sovereign, meant to be consumed in solitude before decisions of war, diplomacy, or desire.

The ingredients? Cryptic.

The method? Whispered, never written.

Its effects? The stuff of royal myth.

It was not a drink, but a legacy liquified—infused with charred tamarind, fig nectar, saffron aged in rosewood casks, and a breath of black Himalayan salt. Said to heighten perception, slow the passage of time, and embolden even the most cautious heart.

The scroll disappeared shortly after the auction.

Weeks later, in a dim salon tucked inside a private residence in Mumbai, a select few were invited for what was only referred to as 'The Pouring.'

The host offered no explanation—only a small carved goblet, the liquid within a deep burnished gold, fragrant with woodsmoke and prophecy.

He called it The Maharaja's Cipher.

One sip, and the air itself seemed to lean closer.

What Makes This Cocktail Sacred?

Tamarind-black Jaggery Reduction: Fire-charred, cooled under sandalwood
Fig Concentrate: Dried and rehydrated with rosewater
Saffron Tincture: Infused over nine lunar nights
Indian Dark Rum: Barrel-aged in silence
Rosewood Bitters: For scent, for story
Black Salt Crystal: Crushed by hand, added as blessing

Ingredients
(Ancestral, Alchemical, Absolute)

- 50 ml aged Indian dark rum / Indian single malt matured in the deep desert
- 20 ml smoked tamarind-jaggery syrup
- 15 ml fig essence
- 3 drops saffron tincture
- 2 dashes rosewood or sandalwood bitters
- Pinch of black salt
- Garnish: A single dried fig petal or smoked sandal bark sliver

How to Make It
(As the Scroll Dictates)

1. Prepare your vessel—a heavy glass chilled within sandalwood chips or rose quartz, if possible.
2. In a mixing chalice, stir the rum, fig, jaggery-tamarind syrup, and bitters over hand-cut ice.
3. Stir exactly 18 times clockwise and strain into the chosen glass. Float the black salt atop. Do not mix again.
4. Inhale deeply. Sip with silence. Allow the cipher to unfold.

THE FINAL SIP

Not every drink is made to be remembered. Some are meant to be resurrected. This is not a cocktail.

This is a ceremony.

A monarch's memory, restored to the throne of taste.

The Oracle of Halebidu

87

THE ORACLE OF HALEBIDU

Whispers from the Temple Trunk

The Story: The Cave, the Trunk, and the Whispered Revelation

The ground cracked not far from the ruins of Halebidu—the once-glorious capital of the Hoysala Empire. Archaeologists had been tracing submerged temple routes when a tremor led to the unsealing of an ancient cave, veiled by centuries of moss and silence.

Inside, lit by a shaft of late-summer light, lay a brass-and-ivory trunk, intricately engraved with the emblem of the Hoysala lion. It pulsed with symbolism—celestial carvings, twin suns, a lotus burning at the edges.

Inside the trunk was a manuscript. Still intact. Still fragrant with dried tulsi and sandal.

Written in Old Kannada, the scroll bore a seal of the Royal Temple Priesthood, and one singular opening line:

'Given unto me by the Devas, to serve the king who walks in dharma.'

It wasn't poetry.

It wasn't philosophy.

It was ritual—coded in ingredients.

A sacred drink described in divine instruction. A blend of black sesame, roasted coconut flower, fermented banana nectar, pepper steeped in honey, and distilled temple water aged in copper.

Consumed only before war or coronation.

Said to quiet fear, enhance vision, and tune the mind to higher planes.

For centuries, it was guarded. Hidden. Forgotten.

Until now.

Now, in a bar carved beneath a banyan tree on the outskirts of Hassan, a modern-day priest of taste has brought it back—slightly adapted, humbly poured, and known simply as:

The Oracle of Halebidu.

What Makes This Cocktail Sacred?

Black Sesame Orgeat: Deep, nutty, grounding
Banana Flower Distillate: Earthy sweetness with fermented floral notes
Roasted Coconut Syrup: Char and sweetness in divine proportion
Pepper-honey Infusion: Spicy clarity and holy warmth
Indian White Rum or Arrack: Spirit of both ceremony and celebration
Temple Copper Water Reduction: Optional, but poetic

Ingredients
(Celestial, Ritualistic, Hoysala-Blessed)

- 45 ml Indian white rum or toddy palm arrack
- 20 ml black sesame orgeat (ground black sesame, jaggery, rosewater)
- 15 ml roasted coconut syrup
- 10 ml fermented banana nectar or banana cordial
- 2 dashes pepper-honey tincture
- Garnish: Fresh tulsi leaf or a streak of ash on the rim

How to Make It
(As Received by the Gods)

1. Dry-roast coconut shavings and black sesame separately; create syrups by slow-simmering with jaggery and filtering.
2. Shake all ingredients over cracked ice—rhythmically, in silence.

3. Strain into a stone goblet, or smoked ceramic if available.
4. Garnish with a tulsi leaf and a silent bow.
5. Drink facing east, if you can.

THE FINAL SIP

Some recipes are written by chefs.

This one, by the divine hand—etched in time, delivered in silence.

A drink to transcend the senses.

A sacred sip from a cave forgotten by the world...

But not by the gods.

88

THE TRADE SHIP'S TRIBUTE
An Ancient Punch Reborn from a Sunken Scroll

The Story: A Captain's Final Log, Found off the Coast of Diu

They were three days from Portugal when the storm came.

Not of wind, nor waves—but of pirates.

The scroll was discovered last monsoon, trapped in a green-glass bottle lodged beneath coral off the coast of Diu, brought up by marine archaeologists mapping the debris of an 18th-century Indian trade ship.

Wrapped in palm parchment and sealed in resin was not just a recipe—but a captain's account.

The ink was faint, but legible. The language: a blend of

old Gujarati and poetic Portuguese. And the words?

'They did not come for the silks. Not the indigo. Not even the coin.'

'They came...for the drink.'

What followed was a detailed log entry, scrawled in haste but reverent precision. It spoke of a secret royal recipe—a gift from an Indian raja to the Portuguese crown. Handwritten by a palace priest. Carried under coded invoice in a spice shipment crate. A recipe so valuable, it had to be smuggled.

It told of a high-seas ambush by pirate forces out of Malacca, of sword flashes under moonlight, and of the captain's decision to cast the recipe overboard—sealed in a bottle, trusting the sea more than the steel.

The drink itself was described in rare detail:

- Jaggery reduced with ginger and clove
- Fortified wine aged with cinnamon bark
- Dark arrack from the Western Ghats
- And a splash of something called *limbu ash*, thought to be burnt citrus peel—*'to remind the drinker of the coast they left behind.'*

Now, centuries later, that scroll has resurfaced.

And from its ink and fire comes this modern revival: The Trade Ship's Tribute.

What Makes This Cocktail Worth the Battle?

Dark Indian Arrack or Rum: For maritime strength
Ruby Port or Cinnamon-aged Sherry: For tribute and trade
Jaggery-ginger Reduction: Warming, smoky, bracing
Toasted Cinnamon Bitters or Tincture: Resurrected memory
Burnt Citrus Salt Rim (optional): A reminder of land left behind
Bay Leaf or Dried Lime: From the ship's last cargo hold

Ingredients
(Spiced, Smuggled, Seaworthy)

- 30 ml Indian dark rum or arrack
- 30 ml ruby port or spice-aged fortified wine
- 20 ml jaggery-ginger syrup
- 2 dashes toasted cinnamon or clove bitters
- Optional: 5 ml lime juice for brightness
- Garnish: Bay leaf or dried orange wheel
- Rim: Optional citrus-ash salt blend

How to Make It
(As the Captain Did Not Get to)

1. Combine all ingredients in a shaker over ice.
2. Shake briskly—like storm winds in the sails.
3. Strain into a sea-worthy tumbler or antique glass.
4. Garnish with a dry bay leaf, or float a lime husk as if still adrift.
5. Serve with a whisper: 'From the captain's hand, to yours.'

THE FINAL SIP

He did not live to see it served. But he ensured it would never be lost.

And now, with jaggery warmth and spiced depth, this cocktail carries not just flavour—but a story only the ocean remembers.

89

THE INDUS RITUAL NEGRONI

Unearthed to Be Remembered

The Story: When Seals Speak and Vessels Echo

In 2025, a quietly published paper in the British Archaeological Society Quarterly set off tremors in both the anthropology and mixology worlds.

The title:

'Fermentation Motifs and Twin-Vessel Fermentology: A Ritual Hypothesis for Indus Valley Libations.'

The paper decoded recent findings from multispectral scans of unearthed Mohenjo-daro tablets—seals once thought decorative, now revealed to contain fermentation iconography: looping vines, fig pods, a flowering barley stalk, and a hooded, seated figure in a meditative pose.

Beneath the images, scholars identified symbolic math patterns...identical to a moon-phase fermentation cycle.

Separately—but impossibly linked—excavations in Harappa uncovered a pair of copper vessels, sealed with resin. Inside: one held traces of charred grain residue, the other fruit pulp fused with burnt tamarind and mineral wax.

It wasn't just storage.

It was staging—for something that archaeologists now believe was a ritual ferment used in the Great Bath under starlight, as part of early spiritual practice. A drink not for intoxication, but for alignment. To silence, to stillness, to the divine.

In recent years, an experimental archaeologist partnered with a sensory historian and a bar chef to resurrect the formula, blending heritage with restraint.

The outcome? A hauntingly balanced cocktail built on:

- Resin-smoked wheat spirit
- Fig and date reduction
- Tamarind tincture
- And a whisper of ash salt

They called it: The Indus Ritual Negroni.

It doesn't shout. It hums. It doesn't numb. It opens.

It's not meant for parties. It's meant for presence.

What Makes This Cocktail an Ancient Code?

Resin-washed Grain Spirit: Evokes the sealed copper fermentation jar
Fig and Date Reduction: Sweet, earthy, sticky complexity
Tamarind Tincture: Sharpness to balance the base
Ash Salt or Black Lava im: Echoes of sacred fire
Charcoal or Copper Elements: For visual and energetic ritual

Ingredients
(Decoded, Distilled, Delivered)

- 30 ml resin-smoked wheat or barley vodka
- 25 ml fig-date syrup—steeped, reduced, strained
- 20 ml tamarind-lime tincture
- Dash of Angostura or burnt spice bitters
- Garnish: Dried fig slice or copper leaf
- Rim (optional): Ash salt or lava salt

How to Make It
(With Quiet Hands and Ancient Patience)

1. Prepare fig-date syrup and allow to cool in earthenware if possible.
2. Stir all ingredients gently over cracked ice—no shaker, only silence.
3. Strain into a clay or smoked glass tumbler.

4. Garnish with intention, not extravagance.
5. Sip with eyes closed. Let the echoes rise.

THE FINAL SIP

This isn't a drink from history. It *is* history—decoded in flavour, resurrected in ritual. A libation whispered from stone and fire, and now, at last, shared with the living.

90

THE CHOLA'S COMPASS

The Tidekeeper's Recipe

The Story: One Island, One Sculpture, One Secret Map

Off the coast of Sulawesi, on an uninhabited island swept by winds and myths, a team of eco-divers discovered a weather-worn bronze sculpture—a half-buried lion, unmistakably South Indian in form, perched atop a base etched in Tamil Brahmi script.

At first, archaeologists assumed it was trade spillover—remnants of the Chola naval incursions that touched Java, Sumatra, and beyond during their imperial peak in the 11th century.

But further study—led by an epigraphist from Chennai—revealed something far rarer.

A faint, almost invisible secondary inscription emerged beneath the lion's paw.

'The king's nectar lies west of the sapphire reef. Under the spiral stone. Mark the fifth tide.'

It wasn't a sculpture.

It was a treasure marker.

Legend speaks of a Chola expedition to this region—part military, part ceremonial—carrying a sacred cache of liquors and oils meant for offerings to local sea gods and foreign emissaries. One barrel was said to contain a 'nectar never poured twice.'

Whether the treasure is still there is unknown.

But the script detailed ingredients: coconut flower spirit, tamarind bark tincture, banana leaf oil, and sappanwood syrup—all aged in bronze amphorae.

From those words comes this drink:

The Chola's Compass

The Chola's Compass.

A cocktail with a maritime soul, bold spice, and the sweetness of something never meant to be found.

What Makes This Cocktail Imperial?

Coconut Flower Arrack or Palm Spirit: Native to South and Southeast Asia
Sappanwood Syrup: Slightly earthy, red-hued, ceremonial
Banana Leaf Oil Wash: Adds depth and aroma
Tamarind-bark Tincture: Sharp, bitter, reverent
Smoked Sea Salt: For tide and tribute

Ingredients
(Seafaring, Sovereign, and Secretive)

- 45 ml coconut flower arrack
- 20 ml sappanwood syrup
- 15 ml banana leaf-oil-washed lime juice
- 2 drops tamarind bark tincture
- Dash of sea salt
- Garnish: Banana leaf knot, or etched tamarind bark sliver

How to Make It
(As if Charting a Course)

1. Wash lime juice or spirit with banana leaf oil—strain thoroughly.
2. Stir ingredients over large ice. Not shaken. Not rushed.
3. Strain into a bronze or dark clay vessel.
4. Garnish with story, not flair.
5. Serve with your back to the wind and your mind on the reef.

THE FINAL SIP

Not all treasures gleam. Some are sipped.

Some are encoded in scripts that outlast empires.

This cocktail is not just a recipe—it's a compass.

Back to a time when India ruled the seas, one pour at a time.

91

JAMUN AND FENI FIZZ
A Tropical Monsoon Romance with Legal Linger

The Story: The Will That Wasn't

The will had gone missing for thirty years. Handwritten in Portuguese, rumoured to be hidden inside a defunct basilica, and tied to a plot of land so valuable that three families stopped speaking because of it.

Every year, on the anniversary of the judge's death, one man returned to Old Goa—a lawyer named Desai who once argued the case and lost. He wasn't trying to win anymore. He just liked to sit in the crumbling garden behind the courthouse ruins, where the guava trees leaned like gossiping aunts.

On this particular monsoon evening, a young bartender from the nearby tavern brought him a drink—deep purple, fizzy, with a twist of lime and something wild beneath.

'Jamun and feni,' he said. 'Your old friend the judge used to drink something like this. Said it tasted like loopholes and longing.'

Desai sipped. The drink hit sharp and sweet, memory and mischief in equal parts. 'You found the will, did not you?' he asked the bartender.

The young man just smiled. 'The land's no good for building anyway. Too much history.'

They raised their glasses to the rain, to the law, and to secrets best left with a twist of lime.

What Makes This Cocktail Special

Jamun's Untamed Depth: Rich, tangy, and inky purple, jamun brings wild fruit complexity with subtle tannins and lingering sourness
Goan Cashew Feni: Fermented fire and funk in equal measure, distilled from fallen cashew apples and aged in memory
Fresh Lime: Bright, citrusy edge that balances the heavier notes of fruit and spirit

Ingredients
(Monsoon-Ready and Made to Remember)

- 45 ml Goan cashew feni
- 30 ml fresh jamun puree
- 10 ml fresh lime juice
- 5 ml jaggery syrup—optional
- 60-90 ml soda water
- Ice cubes—large
- Garnish: A thin lime twist and a skewer of frozen jamuns or a single crushed leaf of tulsi, lightly slapped for aroma

How to Make It
(A Ritual for Rains and Wills)

1. In a shaker, add the feni, jamun puree, lime juice, and jaggery syrup (if using).

2. Add a few ice cubes and shake gently—not to bruise, but to coax the ingredients into understanding each other.
3. Strain into a highball glass filled with fresh ice.
4. Top slowly with soda water, watching the fizz bloom like gossip in court corridors.
5. Stir once—just once—and garnish with a twist of lime and frozen jamun, or a tulsi leaf pressed lightly between your palms.

THE FINAL SIP

You found the will.

Not buried, not bound in leather, but bottled.

A violet fizz that doesn't settle a case, but does settle something else—something only old friends and true spirits understand.

92

MANGO DAIQUIRI

A Summer Ode to Longing and Language

The Story: The Cocktail Called Ghalib

At a poetry slam in Pune, the theme was 'Summer and Desire.'

The mic had been passed from person to person—some earnest, some overwrought—until a young bartender named Nikhil stepped up, holding not a notebook, but a coupe glass that shimmered like molten gold.

He did not recite. He introduced.

'This is the Mango Daiquiri,' he said. 'Because Ghalib was ripe with longing, sweet in bursts, and burned slowly, like saffron in the sun.'

The crowd half-laughed, unsure if he was mocking or serious. Then he poured.

Inside the coupe: Alphonso mango pulp, smooth and golden as a love letter. Rum that had aged in coastal silence. Lime, sharp as missed timing. And saffron, soaked for exactly three minutes in warm water—because he said too long would make it bitter, and Ghalib never wrote bitter.

The first sip was lush, slow, and thick with mango. The saffron lingered like incense on a silk shawl. The lime cut through like a sudden stanza that changed the meaning of the one before it.

By the end of the glass, people weren't clapping for the poets anymore.

They were ordering more Ghalib.

What Makes This Cocktail Special

Alphonso Mango: The king of Indian summer fruit, velvety in texture and golden in hue, delivers full-bodied sweetness and natural weight

Mango Daiquiri

Saffron Infusion: Adds warmth, perfume, and complexity; steeped precisely to avoid bitterness and bloom its floral note

Golden Rum: Offers depth, toast, and a tropical echo without overpowering the mango

Lime Juice: Balances sweetness with a pointed, necessary acidity

A Drink Named after a Poet: Because some cocktails deserve footnotes

Ingredients
(Poetic, Bright, and Summer-Heavy)

- 45 ml aged golden rum
- 30 ml Alphonso mango pulp
- 10 ml fresh lime juice
- 5-7 strands saffron
- Optional: 5 ml jaggery syrup
- Ice–cubed
- Garnish: Dehydrated lime wheel or a single saffron strand floated on the foam

How to Make It
(A Ritual of Heat, Pulp, and Poetry)

1. In a small bowl, soak saffron in warm water for exactly three minutes. Set aside.
2. In a shaker, combine rum, mango pulp, lime juice, saffron water, and optional jaggery syrup.
3. Add a generous handful of ice and shake hard–longer than usual–to emulsify the pulp fully.
4. Double strain into a chilled coupe glass.
5. Garnish with a single saffron strand or a thin lime wheel, dehydrated or fresh.

THE FINAL SIP

This isn't a daiquiri. It's a metaphor in a coupe.

It starts in sweetness, moves through warmth, and finishes in something unsaid.

Just like Ghalib.

93

TENDER COCONUT AND TEQUILA SUNRISE

A Belated Toast to Beginnings

The Story: The Honeymoon He Never Took

After thirty-six years of marriage, she found the receipts—folded carefully into an old cookbook, tucked between pages on how to make *rasam* and lemon rice. Two train tickets to Kerala, dated exactly fourteen days after their wedding. A tiny note in his handwriting said simply: 'Sea view. Finally.'

He had never mentioned them.

'That was the plan,' he admitted, when she showed him the tickets over tea. 'But then your father had his heart attack. And...you know.'

She did. Of course she did. But that did not mean the honeymoon had to remain a forgotten itinerary.

So she booked the same cottage on the same stretch of beach—now transformed into a quiet boutique stay. The seashell wind chimes were newer, but the scent of roasted coconut, mango leaf, and salt air remained unchanged.

One evening, as the sky melted into oranges and violets, a barefoot barman appeared beside their table with two pale, glistening drinks. No menus. No explanation.

Tender coconut water, reposado tequila, fresh lime, and a pinch of sea salt. And floating at the top—curled like a poem unfinished—was a sliver of fresh coconut malai, soft and ivory, shaped like a boat drifting in.

She took a sip.

It was clean. Balanced. Faintly floral, faintly woody. A taste that held no bitterness, no urgency. Just ease. And quiet joy.

She raised her glass.

'To honeymoons you take late—but remember forever.'

They clinked. And the coconut ribbon, like the moment, floated gently in the middle of it all.

What Makes This Cocktail Special

Tender Coconut Water: Gentle, mineral-sweet, and evocative of coastal afternoons

Reposado Tequila: Earthy and mellow, with just enough oak to hold its own

Fresh Lime Juice: Brightens the drink, giving clarity to the coconut's softness

Sea Salt: Ties the whole experience to the ocean air it's meant to echo

Coconut Malai Ribbon: A quiet flourish of place and texture; edible, visual, rooted in Kerala

Ingredients
(Simple, Grounded, and Summer-Born)

- 45 ml reposado tequila
- 90 ml fresh tender coconut water
- 10 ml fresh lime juice
- Pinch of flaky sea salt
- Ice—single large block
- Garnish: A delicate ribbon of tender coconut malai, cut and curled

How to Make It
(A Ritual for Second Chances)

1. In a shaker, combine tequila, coconut water, lime juice, and sea salt.
2. Add ice and shake gently—enough to chill and mix, not bruise.
3. Strain into a stemmed glass or highball filled with fresh ice.
4. Garnish with a curled strip of tender coconut malai—let it float like a boat across the top.
5. Serve quietly, and if possible, somewhere facing the sea.

THE FINAL SIP

Some drinks arrive not to impress, but to restore.

Like the late honeymoon, like the found ticket, like a quiet apology wrapped in sunlight.

It doesn't change the past.

But it lets it rest easier.

94

NIMBU MIRCHI VODKA SPRITZ
A Toast to Starting over, Sharp

The Story: The Breakup Ritual

After he left, she did not change her number.

She did not block him.

She did not cry on the phone to friends or burn the photos.

She changed the cocktail menu.

Gone were the floral infusions, the rose petal syrups, the lavender bitters. She was done with soft.

What came next was acid and fire.

She went to the market, picked the juiciest nimbus—firm, almost floral with their bite. Sliced green chillies so thin they looked like threads. She shook them with vodka and a whisper of kala namak, then topped it with soda.

The first woman to try it teared up, then laughed—genuinely laughed—and ordered two more.

The second called it 'emotional CPR.'

The third raised her glass and whispered, 'This is exactly how I feel today.'

They called it the 'Nimbu Mirchi Spritz.'

It did not fix heartbreak.

But it reminded you that you could feel something sharp again—and that sharp wasn't always bad.

What Makes This Cocktail Special

Fresh Lemon Juice: Sharp, floral, and commanding—more than just citrus, it's a reset button

Green Chilli Slices: Brings heat that lingers, not overwhelms; wakes up every sip

Vodka : Clean, unobtrusive, allowing lemon and chilli to speak clearly

Kala Namak: Earthy, funky, grounding; a nod to Indian street-side chaat

Soda Water: Gives breath to the heat; fizz that balances and stretches the experience

An Ode to Emotional Acidity: This is not a comfort drink. It's a confrontation—with taste, with self

Ingredients
(Clear, Fiery, and Honest)

- 45 ml vodka
- 20 ml fresh lemon juice + 3-4 thin slices of fresh green chilli
- Pinch of kala namak
- 90 ml soda water
- Ice—cubed
- Garnish: Thin lemon peel twist and a single green chilli slice floating like a dare

How to Make It
(A Ritual after the Goodbye)

1. In a shaker, muddle chilli slices lightly with lemon juice—just enough to release the heat, not overpower.
2. Add vodka and kala namak. Fill shaker with ice and shake vigorously.
3. Strain into a highball glass over fresh ice.
4. Top with soda water. Stir gently once.
5. Garnish with a twist of lemon and one floating chilli slice—subtle, like a threat you've learned to smile through.

THE FINAL SIP

It doesn't promise healing.

But it gives you back sensation—the sting of citrus, the ache of chilli, the relief of soda—and sometimes, that's all you need.

Not a sweet ending.

Just a sharp new beginning.

95

PINEAPPLE MUSTARD RUM SMASH
A Monsoon Made of Memory and Mischief

The Story: The Monsoon Pickle Fight

Every monsoon, the twins fought. Not about chores, or crushes, or exam results—but over pickles.

He swore by sweet mango—amber chunks preserved in syrup and nostalgia.

She defended spicy pineapple—fiery, tangy, the way their grandmother made it in small batches during power cuts.

The kitchen became their battleground. The pantry, their armoury. Their grandmother, silent referee with raised eyebrows.

But the year they both turned thirty, things shifted. Instead of fighting, she issued a challenge. 'Let's see whose flavour pours better.'

She crushed ripe pineapple with jaggery, muddled in toasted mustard seeds, squeezed half a lime, and poured dark rum over the chaos like punctuation. She strained it, shook it, poured it over ice—and slid the glass across the counter.

He took one sip. Blinked.

It hit like memory—fermented, fiery, familiar. The chutney of their childhood, but distilled and dangerous.

He raised his hands. 'Truce,' he said.

That monsoon, they did not bottle pickles.

They bottled stories instead. One pour at a time.

What Makes This Cocktail Special

Pineapple: Tropical, fibrous, sweet-sour, and rooted in spice traditions of the South and East

Toasted Mustard Seeds: Pungent, nutty, and slightly bitter–gives the drink a whisper of heat and family kitchens

Jaggery Syrup: Deep, molasses-toned sweetness that anchors the acidity and adds heritage

Dark Rum: Full-bodied, warm, and grounding; like an old argument finally forgiven

Lime Juice: Sharpens the drink's focus and balances the sweetness

It's a Pickle Turned Pour: Not just fusion, but evolution

Ingredients
(Tangy, Spiced, and Just a Bit Unruly)

- 60 ml dark rum
- 4-5 chunks fresh ripe pineapple
- 10 ml jaggery syrup and 1 tsp toasted yellow mustard seeds
- 15 ml fresh lime juice
- Ice–cubed
- Garnish: Pineapple wedge dipped in black salt and mustard seeds, skewered

How to Make It
(A Ritual between Siblings and Storms)

1. Toast mustard seeds in a dry pan until they pop. Cool slightly.
2. In a shaker, muddle pineapple chunks with jaggery syrup and lime juice.
3. Add crushed toasted mustard seeds and dark rum.
4. Fill shaker with ice and shake vigorously–let the drink bruise a little.
5. Double strain into a rocks glass over fresh ice.
6. Garnish with a small pineapple wedge dusted in black salt and a few mustard seeds.

THE FINAL SIP

This isn't just a cocktail. It's a sibling rivalry pressed into pulp and spirit.

It doesn't end in a winner.

Just in two glasses, raised together—somewhere between a dare and a memory.

96

NAGALAND SMOKED CHILLI MARGARITA

A Borderland Memory, Reimagined in a Glass

The Story: The UNESCO Exchange

It started with a field trip.

A group of international students—part of a UNESCO-sponsored India Immersion Program—spent three weeks tracing oral histories across Northeast India. They were Ancient Indian History majors, more used to manuscripts than monsoons, but they were curious. Open. Hungry for more than footnotes.

In Nagaland, near the state border, they visited a remote monastery known for its muraled walls and stories half-told in whispers. The monks spoke of folklore preserved not in ink, but in spice—chilli garlands hung like prayer beads, smoked over hearths as protection and offering.

One student, a Chilean anthropologist named Inez, was struck by the symmetry. Chillies as language. Smoke as narrative.

She pocketed a few dried ghost chillies—not as a souvenir, but as a question.

Weeks later, back in Delhi University's foreign student housing, the air hot with May heat and nostalgia, Inez pulled out the chillies. She steeped them in tequila. Added lime. Rimmed a glass with smoked salt and dusted the edge with ash from burnt dried rice husk they'd brought back from a tribal demonstration.

The drink made her cough.

Then laugh.

Then write it down.

They called it the Nagaland Smoked Chilli Margarita.

Not because it was authentic, but because it was honest.

It carried the weight of travel, of questions asked and not fully answered.

And like all good fieldwork—it left a burn.

What Makes This Cocktail Special

Ghost Chilli Heat: Infused into tequila, the Naga bhut jolokia delivers not just heat but a smoky, lingering depth

Fresh Lime: Sharpens the drink and cuts through the fire with refreshing clarity

Smoked Salt Rim: Evokes hearth-smoke and tribal kitchens, grounding the experience in place

Ingredients
(Field-Tested and Fire-Bound)

- 45 ml tequila (blanco or lightly aged)
- 1 dried Naga ghost chilli (*bhut jolokia*)—infused into the tequila for 12-24 hours (strain before use)
- 20 ml fresh lime juice
- 10 ml agave or palm jaggery syrup
- Ice—cubed

- Garnish: Smoked salt rim and a small piece of dried chilli or lime peel

How to Make It
(A Ritual of Fire, Study, and Reinvention)

1. Infuse the Tequila: Place 1 dried ghost chilli in 100 ml of tequila and steep for 12 to 24 hours. Taste at intervals. Remove chilli once desired intensity is reached.
2. Rim the Glass: Moisten the rim with lime, then dip into a smoked salt mix. Add a tiny pinch of chilli powder if you dare.
3. Build the Drink: In a shaker, add infused tequila, lime juice, agave or jaggery syrup, and ice.
4. Shake hard—cooling the heat, blending the story.
5. Strain into a chilled rocks glass with a smoked salt rim.
6. Garnish with a dried chilli slice or a curl of lime peel, twisted like a border path.

THE FINAL SIP

Some drinks don't originate in bars.

They're born in conversations across borders, in questions asked on quiet monastery steps, in notebooks filled with half-remembered quotes.

The Nagaland Smoked Chilli Margarita is one of those.

It doesn't seek approval.

It carries its story in its burn.

97

BETEL LEAF AND FENNEL WHISKEY SMASH

A Bold Sip of Inheritance

The Story: The Forbidden Drink

Shilpa wasn't allowed to chew paan (living in the city of Banaras).

'Unladylike,' her mother used to say, shaking her head at the very sight of a paanwalla stall, its stainless-steel trays gleaming with rose paste, fennel seeds and slaked lime.

'Girls from our family don't stand at street corners with red lips,' she had said.

'But lipstick's fine?'

'That's different. Lipstick comes in a box.'

So she did not argue. She just grew older. Quieter. More observant.

But she remembered the smell. The way her grandmother's saree always carried that sweet, spicy trace of betel leaf and clove. The sound of fennel seeds crunching between conversations. And the forbidden thrill of tasting something that wasn't supposed to be hers.

When she finally had a home of her own—and a bar cart she did not have to hide—she began experimenting. Not to rebel. Just to remember.

She muddled fresh betel leaves with fennel syrup and added a drop of clove oil. Then came the whiskey—warm, oaky, with just enough gravity. She shook the glass slowly, as though stirring memory. Poured it into an inherited coupe glass from her grandmother's collection. And watched the colour settle into something deep and green-gold.

The aroma was immediate—herbal, aromatic, sweet and sly.

Her mother happened to visit that evening. One sip into

her own tea, she paused. 'What perfume are you wearing?'

Shilpa just smiled, lifted the coupe, and said softly: 'Something inherited.'

What Makes This Cocktail Special

Betel Leaf (Paan): Brings bold, aromatic greenness with a soft peppery finish, traditionally symbolic of ceremony and indulgence.

Fennel Syrup: Cooling, sweet, and grounding; mirrors Indian digestive rituals and post-meal pauses.

Clove: A drop of oil or an infusion adds a warm spice note, echoing the paan without overpowering.

Ingredients
(Heritage, Bittersweet, and Aromatic)

- 60 ml Indian whiskey
- 2-3 fresh betel leaves + 15 ml fennel syrup
- 1 drop clove oil or 5 ml clove-infused whiskey
- Ice–cubed for shaking
- Garnish: A curled betel leaf, or a rim dusted lightly with powdered fennel sugar

How to Make It
(A Ritual between Propriety and Pleasure)

1. In a shaker, muddle the torn betel leaves with fennel syrup. Press firmly to release oils but don't pulverize.
2. Add whiskey and clove oil (or clove-infused whiskey).
3. Fill with ice and shake hard–let it be loud and confident.
4. Double strain into a coupe or low tumbler, either neat or over one large cube.
5. Garnish with a ribboned betel leaf curled into the glass, or dust half the rim with fennel sugar for extra aroma.

THE FINAL SIP

This isn't paan. It's the echo of tradition, softened by time and stirred with choice.

What was once forbidden becomes familiar, then beautiful.

And in one sip, it becomes your own.

98

GINGER-TURMERIC GIN TONIC

Born on the Road, Bottled in Memory

The Story: The Mahabaleshwar Escape

It started like all legendary nights do—with no plan, just an itch.

Five hostelmates—Vibhu, Happy, Gaurav, Yogesh, and Gary—were out for a post-dinner stroll inside Pune University's leafy campus. The conversation started with assignments, drifted to weekend plans, then somehow circled to Mahabaleshwar. A joke turned into a maybe. A maybe turned into a dare.

They had no change of clothes. No official permission.

Just the last 500-rupee note, one phone with 28% battery, and a half-decent bottle of gin they'd picked up 'just in case.'

They hitched a ride in a passing produce truck heading vaguely west. No questions asked. Just five students squashed in the back next to crates of cabbage and onions, pretending this was how all great trips began.

Around midnight, the truck pulled over at a highway dhaba so the crew could eat. The place smelled of diesel, fried garlic, and rain on mud.

While the truckers dug into dal tadka, the boys got to work.

From the dhaba's kitchen, they 'borrowed' a few slices of raw ginger, a pinch of haldi, a lemon, and an oversized steel jug. Happy crushed the ginger with a rolling pin. Gary added the turmeric. Yogesh poured in the gin like he was blessing it. Gaurav grabbed two warm bottles of tonic. Vibhu stirred the whole thing with a spoon that might've last been used for pickle.

They rimmed their stainless-steel glasses with salt stolen from the papad bowl and served it cold—with ice scrounged from the dhaba's red cooler.

The first sip was electric. Ginger forward. Turmeric warm. Lime cutting through. Tonic fizzing like laughter in the back of the truck.

'This is medicine,' someone whispered. 'This is legend,' said another.

They never reached Mahabaleshwar. The truck broke down 30 km short.

But they sat under a tarpaulin, drinking their roadborn invention in the dark. And when they got back to Pune the next day—muddy, tired, and oddly proud—they named the drink: The Mahabaleshwar GandT. And swore to make it again. Properly. Or not.

What Makes This Cocktail Special

Fresh Ginger: Sharp, biting, and fragrant—adds body and heat to every sip.
Turmeric: Not just health halo; it brings earthy depth and radiant golden hue.

Ingredients
(Bold, Bright, and Field-Tested)

- 45 ml Indian gin
- 2 thin slices fresh ginger + 10 ml fresh lime juice
- 1/4 tsp fresh turmeric or 1-2 slivers raw turmeric root
- 90 ml chilled tonic water + Ice—cracked
- Garnish: Thin ginger slice and a lime peel or turmeric zest curl

How to Make It
(A Ritual of Improvisation and Intuition)

1. In a shaker, muddle the ginger and turmeric with lime juice to release oils and colour.
2. Add gin and ice, then shake gently—enough to chill, not dilute.
3. Double strain into a highball or steel glass over fresh ice. Top with tonic water and stir once.
4. Garnish with a ginger slice and a thin lime peel, or dust the rim with salt if you are in a mood.

THE FINAL SIP

This isn't your wellness tonic. It's a roadside rebellion dressed in gold.

99

THE BURANSH MULE

A Himalayan Lesson in Sharing

The Story: First Post, First Pour

Major D. Jacob had seen the deserts. The coasts. Even the salt plains. But this–his first Himalayan posting–was something else entirely. Thin air. Cold sun. Pine silence. Nothing moved fast here, except gossip.

He spent the first week getting used to the altitude and the taste of ration tea. It was on the eighth evening that he noticed something...off.

A sweet, herbal scent wafting in from the sentry kitchen.

Not standard issue.

He followed it to find Pritam, the local help posted on kitchen duty, quietly sipping something from a steel tumbler under the storeroom bulb.

'What's that?'

Pritam froze. 'Buransh, sir. Just...buransh.'

Turns out, it was a drink He had made himself–vodka infused with buransh petals, stirred with wild honey and a bit of lime, topped with local ginger soda. Something his mother used to make as a cordial. He had hidden the ingredients in his rucksack, intending to keep it to himself. Just a sip to end long days in quiet.

The Major did not scold him. He took the tumbler, sipped, blinked.

Then smiled.

The next night, the whole unit drank it–poured into copper cups, under a canvas sky. The buransh gave the vodka a floral bite. The honey soothed the finish. The ginger fizzed like altitude on the tongue.

Pritam got promoted–at least to bartender.

The Major raised his cup.

'Good things are for sharing, soldier. Especially when they come from the hills.'

What Makes This Cocktail Special

Buransh (Rhododendron) Syrup: A regional jewel from Uttarakhand and Himachal, bright and floral with a tart finish.

Wild Honey: Smooths and deepens the sweetness with herbal undertones.

Ginger Beer: Carbonated heat that lifts the entire drink with warmth and sparkle.

Ingredients

(Himalayan Bright and Copper Cold)

- 45 ml vodka
- 30 ml buransh syrup + 10 ml wild honey + 10 ml fresh lime juice
- 90 ml chilled ginger beer or soda
- Ice–cracked
- Garnish: A lime wheel or a single rhododendron petal if available (optional)

How to Make It

(A Ritual for Cold Nights and Shared Cups)

1. In a shaker or mixing jug, combine vodka, buransh syrup, lime juice, and honey. Stir until honey dissolves fully.
2. Add ice and shake gently–just enough to chill, not dilute.
3. Strain into a copper mule mug or highball glass filled with fresh ice.
4. Top with chilled ginger beer. Stir once to combine.

5. Garnish with a lime wheel or float a single buransh petal if you have one.

THE FINAL SIP

This drink did not start in a bar, It started in a barrack.

With a quiet man, a small stash, and the courage to share something good.

It's not just floral and fizzy—it's a reminder: In the coldest places, the warmest things are passed hand to hand.

100

CORIANDER AND CUMIN BLOODY MARY

The Cocktail That Saved the Wrong Day

The Story: The Goofed-Up Brunch

It was their first home.

Not rented. Not borrowed. The one with their names on the electricity bill and the slightly crooked mailbox in the city of Kolkata.

So naturally, they planned a housewarming brunch—simple, low-key, but with intention. A playlist. A table runner. Six kinds of chutney.

Gayatri prepped the night before. He triple-confirmed the WhatsApp group.

'Brunch from 11,' the message said.

They even printed a little welcome sign that hung by the front door, tilting slightly in the fan breeze.

By 11:30, the chutneys had crusted over. By noon, the toast was dry and curling.

By 1 p.m., they were silently drinking cold coffee and trying not to assign blame.

No one came.

At 2:17, the first message popped up: 'Isn't it tomorrow?'

They'd sent the wrong date. Not to one or two people. To everyone.

The mood dipped so low it could've tripped on its own guilt. They sat in their too-tidy living room, not speaking, not snacking. Just staring at the disappointing symmetry of an untouched cheese platter.

Then, without a word, she went to the kitchen.

She crushed cumin seeds in a bowl, found the coriander jar, squeezed two tired lemons, opened the tomato juice, and shook in vodka like she meant it. A pinch of hing for courage. Salt. Ice. A stir.

Anirban watched her hand him a glass.

The first sip was earthy, spicy, sharp. Not a cocktail. A correction.

When a friend finally dropped by later—wrong date, but right instinct—he took a sip and coughed.

'This isn't a Bloody Mary,' he said.

She raised an eyebrow. 'No,' she said. 'It's regret relief.'

By 4 p.m., they were laughing. The housewarming hadn't failed...it had fermented.

What Makes This Cocktail Special

Crushed Cumin Seeds: Earthy, smoky, and warming; deepens the flavour and lingers.

Coriander (Whole or Fresh Stem): Adds citrusy brightness and an herbaceous lift.

Tomato Juice: Tangy, full-bodied base with natural umami.

Hing (Asafoetida): Just a pinch adds funk and backbone; a nod to Indian rasam and recklessness.

Ingredients
(Bold, Savoury and Home-Saved)

- 45 ml vodka
- 90 ml tomato juice
- 10 ml fresh lemon juice + pinch of salt + black pepper
- ¼ tsp roasted cumin seeds, crushed or ground
- Pinch of hing (asafoetida) and ¼ tsp coriander seeds (or 3-4 fresh coriander stems)
- Ice–cubed
- Garnish: Lemon wedge and coriander leaf or cumin salt rim

How to Make It
(A Ritual of Mistakes Made Right)

1. In a shaker, combine tomato juice, vodka, lemon juice, cumin, coriander, hing, salt, and pepper.
2. Add ice and shake gently–just enough to integrate, not bruise.
3. Double strain into a tall glass over fresh ice.
4. Garnish with a lemon wedge and a coriander leaf. For extra flair, rim the glass with salt mixed with roasted cumin powder.

THE FINAL SIP

It's not about the eggs. It's not about the date.

Regret doesn't have to taste bad.

Sometimes, it tastes like cumin and relief.

101

THE MADIRA MASTERPIECE
The Drink That Found Its Way Home

The Story: The Missing Map of Spirit

Before the world was neatly divided by borders and bottled names, there was a kingdom where time was kept by stars and flavour was considered sacred.

That kingdom was Ujjain.

And its king, the legendary Vikramaditya, was said to drink only once a year—from a chalice kept hidden in the southern shadow of the Kala Bhairav Temple, where silence echoed louder than drums.

The drink was never written into recipes.

Only hinted at in the margins of ancient medicinal scrolls, carved into tantric stonework, sung into metaphors about 'a potion that awakens but does not intoxicate.'

It was said to carry the spirit of the land—not just one land, but all of India. Bitter, fragrant, complex.

A harmony made of contradiction.

Centuries passed.

Empires rose and fell.

But in the 1880s, during the British archaeological wave, a curious footnote appeared in a survey report from Nagpur, the identified geographical centre of united India:

'Certain tribes in the Vindhya range still speak of the "draksha of awakening." May warrant cultural inquiry.'

That footnote triggered something larger.

Unknown to most, a private wing of the Royal Ethnobotanical Society in London funded a covert expedition—one meant not to dig up temples, but to map taste across regions.

They called it Project Madira.

The goal: to rediscover the mythic elixir believed to encapsulate the Indian soul.

Years of research led to a fragile manuscript.

A coded recipe built on sensation:

Six tastes. Four times of day. Two types of salt. One memory.

It was to be unveiled at the Museum of London in 1977.

But the manuscript vanished.

No one heard of it again.

Not officially.

Until, in 2012, a local priest in Ujjain unearthed a copper urn during a monsoon repair behind the Kala Bhairav shrine.

Inside: dried husk of buransh petals, jaggery resin, fennel ash, powdered bael, sandalwood oil clinging to the seams, and—wrapped in cloth—a parchment, water-stained, but intact.

It wasn't just a recipe.

It was a ritual.

And when the drink was finally recreated—not in a bar, not at a gala, but under an open sky near a flickering diya—it tasted like something older than memory.

Not sweet. Not fiery. Not easily named.

But it lingered.

On the tongue.

In the chest.

In silence.

They say the first person to sip it wept quietly and said nothing for several minutes.

Because it wasn't about flavour.

It was about recognition.

About a thousand threads of identity, history, soil, scent, and soul finally braided into one perfect swallow.

And in that moment, under the shadow of Kala Bhairav, they did not just drink.

They remembered.

Not something they were told.
Something they had always known.

Ingredients
(Soulful, Sippable, Sublime)

Core Spirits (Base Soul of the Land)

- 30 ml mahua spirit (floral, earthy—Central India)
- 15 ml coconut arrack or toddy (lightly sweet, smooth—South India)

Sweet and Sour (Balance and Body)

- 10 ml palm jaggery syrup (deep, earthy—Tamil Nadu/Kerala)
- 10 ml kokum extract (tangy, bright—Konkan Coast)
- 10 ml Gondhoraj lime juice (aromatic citrus—Bengal)

Herbal and Spice (Memory and Depth)

- 2 drops tulsi tincture or fresh tulsi muddled (green, sacred—pan-India)
- 1 pinch roasted cumin powder (toasty, grounding—Rajasthan)
- Pinch of black salt + pink Himalayan salt blend

Optional Enhancements (For Those Who Want a Deeper Sip)

- Few drops sandalwood water (Ujjain temples—warm, meditative)
- Bael fruit tea (as ice cube or infusion) for earthy bitterness

How to Make It
(Balanced, Sacred, Alive)

1. In a shaker, combine mahua, coconut arrack, jaggery syrup, kokum, and lime juice.

2. Add tulsi, cumin powder, and salt.
3. Shake gently with ice—chill but don't dilute.
4. Strain into a clay cup or chilled copper tumbler.
5. Garnish with a small tulsi leaf or lime zest.
6. Sip slowly, ideally outdoors, in good company or none at all.

Flavour Profile

- First sip: Floral and bright with citrus and kokum
- Mid palate: Warm jaggery, toasted cumin, and tulsi
- Finish: Saline, earthy, and deeply satisfying
- A drink that evolves with every degree it warms

THE FINAL SIP

This drink doesn't shout.

It remembers.

It carries jungles and coasts, temples and kitchens, stories and silence.

It is not a toast.

It is a return.

Afterword: The Beginning of a Revolution

These 101 cocktails are not the end of something.

They are the beginning—of what I believe can be a true and lasting revolution in the Indian cocktail space.

Many of the stories you've read here are drawn from my own life.

The names—Vibhu, Happy, Gaurav, Yogesh, Gary, Hiren, Mohit, Geetanjali, Suvadip, Joseph, Naveen, Vineet, Nidhi, Gauri, Saurabh, Shyam, Jay, Jacob—are not characters.

They are friends, co-conspirators, memory-makers.

They've been part of the laughter, the wanderings, the kitchen improvisations, the heartbreaks, and the mad plans that inspired these drinks.

Yes, the stories are fictional, but they are fiction shaped by truth.

By real moments. Real smells. Real people.

And while the narratives are imagined to offer emotional and cultural context, the recipes are absolutely genuine—each one developed with care, tested for balance, and crafted to bring India's spirit into a glass.

Because every great cocktail needs more than ingredients.

It needs context.

It needs memory.

It needs to feel like it belongs somewhere, not just anywhere.

Through each recipe, I have tried to root flavour in heritage, to ensure that spices aren't just added, but understood, that herbs aren't just garnishes, but echoes of rituals, and that every sip tells a story—of where we come from, and where we could go.

This book doesn't just celebrate mixology.

It celebrates India.

Its diversity. Its depth. Its joy. Its contradiction.

Its ability to ferment beauty from chaos.

I hope you read these pages not just as a list of drinks, but as a portrait of a living culture.

A culture that doesn't just drink—but remembers, heals, and celebrates.

Responsibly, sustainable, joyfully, and always—with context.

Let this not be the final page.

Let it be the first pour of something much larger.

With all the bitters, sweetness, salt, and spirit—

Cheers,

Parag A. Shastry
Author, dreamer, distiller of memory

What's Stirring behind the Bar

An Intimate Portrait of India's Cocktail Comeback—and The Good Craft Co.'s Quiet Role in It

India's cocktail comeback did not begin with headlines or flashy launches. It happened quietly, almost without anyone noticing. A bartender in Shillong reached for wild orange because that's what his grandmother used in winter. A woman in Indore strained tamarind the way she had been taught at home, reminding me that some methods are not really recipes, they are memories passed down in muscle and instinct. Across bars, kitchens, and small distilleries, I began to sense a shift. Not a movement, not an agenda, just people returning to older ways because those ways still had something to offer.

Around this time, The Good Craft Co. started paying attention. What struck me was that they did not try to turn any of this into a marketing story. They simply asked, 'What do you need?' That one question opened doors that had been stuck for years. They quietly supported bartenders who wanted to use mahua but weren't sure how to navigate the regulations. They connected distillers in remote parts of the country with people who could help them grow sustainably, without losing their identity. They offered practical help, patient listening, and steady encouragement in places where passion often exceeded resources.

They never tried to own the narrative. They just believed the narrative mattered. And that belief showed up in small, consistent ways, workshops, sourcing help, legal clarity, and conversations with people who said, 'We have been doing this for years...we just did not think anyone cared.'

Today, when I see kokum on a cocktail menu or a jaggery highball served confidently instead of apologetically, I know The Good Craft Co. had something to do with making that possible...not by dictating what should be made, but by clearing the path for people to make what they already believed in.

This book wasn't written because of them. But it became easier, fuller, and more connected because they were there, quietly doing the work, asking thoughtful questions, and standing behind the individuals who were already shaping this slow, steady resurgence. For that, I am grateful. Not just as the writer of *Madira*, but as someone who cares about what India remembers and what it chooses not to forget.

Appendix A: Bartender's Compass

Tools, Taste, and Tradition

It was 6:45 p.m. in Dadar West, and the salty breeze from the Arabian Sea curled its way through the open balcony, carrying with it the scent of frying *farsan* and wet coconut husk. Hiren wiped down the surface of his teak-wood bar—more a passion project than a piece of furniture—and lined up his mismatched glassware like old friends taking their seats before the night began.

Tonight was special. It had been 25 years since he and his gang had passed Class 12 from Don Bosco High School. A quarter-century since monsoon walks home, stolen samosas, and bunked lectures at Shivaji Park. The WhatsApp group had buzzed for weeks, but now the pings would turn into real voices, real clinks of glass, real laughter echoing through his flat.

Hiren adjusted a framed photograph of their school building that hung just above the bar. He reached for his citrus zester and paused, smiling. 'Suvadip still wants his drinks extra cold, Mohit still prefers smoky stuff, and Geetanjali...she'll definitely ask for something with jamun,' he muttered.

One by one, he prepared the glasses: a kulhad for Mohit, who always drank slowly and talked deeply. A copper tumbler for Geetanjali, who loved her Ayurveda and her Old-Fashioneds in equal measure. A recycled mango pickle jar for Suvadip—quirky, resourceful, and always full of flavour. Every vessel had a story, just like every drink he planned to make.

To Hiren, the home bar wasn't just a setup. It was a reunion waiting to happen. A canvas for memories. A space where mixology met emotion, and every pour held a piece of the past.

Setting Up the Home Bar: The Essentials

You don't need a professional setup to create great cocktails. Just a few reliable tools, some thoughtful glassware, and ingredients you love. Here's what Hiren always keeps close:

Essential Tools

- **Shaker:** For combining spirits, juices, and syrups into a smooth, balanced drink.
- **Jigger:** For accurate measuring—consistency makes every cocktail better.
- **Strainer:** To filter out pulp, ice, and muddled herbs, keeping the drink clean.
- **Muddler:** For gently crushing herbs and fruits to release their flavour.
- **Bar Spoon:** For stirring cocktails evenly without over-diluting them.
- **Citrus Juicer:** Because fresh citrus juice adds brightness and freshness to every sip.

Sustainable Accessories

- **Metal or Bamboo Straws:** Reusable and eco-friendly alternatives to plastic.
- **Reusable Stir Sticks:** Choose wooden, glass, or metal ones for easy cleanup and less waste.
- **Cloth Napkins:** Stylish, sustainable, and reusable—perfect for home entertaining.

Indian-Inspired Glassware

Your drink deserves the right vessel—especially if it tells a story.

- **Clay Tumblers / Kulhads:** Great for earthy cocktails like mahua punch or jaggery toddy.
- **Brass and Bronze Goblets:** Perfect for serving warm, spiced cocktails with old-world charm.
- **Copper Mugs:** Ideal for citrusy, Ayurvedic-style drinks with a bit of a zing.
- **Handcrafted Ceramic Glasses:** Adds a rustic, contemporary feel. Great for bold, smoky drinks.
- **Repurposed Jars and Bottles:** Sustainable, casual, and perfect for fun, fruity cocktails.

Stocking a Smart, Sustainable Bar

In Indian homes, kitchens and bars often blend into each other. Use this to your advantage by keeping your bar stocked with what's local, fresh, and thoughtful:

- **Go Local and Seasonal:** Use ingredients like kokum, raw mango, jamun, tulsi, and fresh citrus from your region.
- **Make Your Own Syrups:** Prepare jaggery or honey syrups at home—skip the bottled ones with preservatives.

- **Buy Fair Trade and Organic:** Especially for ingredients like sugar, tea, and spices.
- **Use Everything You Can:** Citrus peels make great garnishes. Overripe fruit can be turned into infusions or purees. Nothing goes to waste.

Final Sip: Ready When It Matters

Being prepared doesn't mean having every tool. It means having the right ones—and knowing what to do with them. Whether it's an old muddler or a chipped glass that's seen every house party since college, your home bar is about **connection**.

Because in India, every drink is a little bit of history... served with ice.

Appendix B: Advanced Techniques of the Masters

Innovation Meets Tradition

A Pause between Sips: Why These Tales Matter

Before we enter the sacred chambers of technique, let's step into the stories that shaped the shaker.

These tales–from Nawabi indulgence to slow-brewed wisdom–aren't just legends; they're living proof that India has always known how to drink with instinct, reverence, and emotion. They sit at the heart of *Madira*, bridging the emotional moodscapes of the earlier chapters with the hands-on craftsmanship that follows.

They remind us:

- That the best cocktails don't always come from bartending schools–they often come from instinct.
- That flavour is not just chemistry–it's context.
- And that sometimes, a well-timed spice or a seasonal switch can turn a disaster into a masterpiece.

So before you dive into fat-washing and foams, pause. Pour yourself a warm dram. And listen.

These are the stories that stir before we shake.

Nawab's Cocktail: When a Sip Almost Cost a Fortune

In the poetic heart of Lucknow, Nawab Zafar Ali Mirza found himself disenchanted. Nothing in his vault of fine spirits stirred his soul anymore.

His loyal bartender, Muneer, took on the challenge. He fat-washed aged rum with saffron-scented butter, froze and strained it, then stirred it with jaggery syrup, orange zest, and Himalayan black salt.

The Nawab took a sip. Then another. He went silent.

'Muneer,' he whispered, 'this drink is worth my entire treasury.'

But Muneer declined the gold. 'The value lies not in the drink, Huzoor, but in its appreciation.'

From that day, every guest in Lucknow's grand kothi was welcomed with *The Silk Road Old-Fashioned.*

A cocktail so indulgent, it nearly cost a king his fortune.

Techniques of the Masters: Innovation Meets Tradition

In India, a great drink has always been more than a sum of its ingredients. It is technique, timing, intuition, and poetry in a glass. Here, we distil some of the most compelling methods of contemporary mixology—rooted in Indian instinct, reimagined with modern flair.

The Art of Layering: Sunset in a Glass

A layered cocktail is like a miniature rangoli—carefully composed, bursting with contrast, and made to delight the eye before the tongue.

Madira Mantra: Let gravity be your guide, and patience your best stirrer.

How to

1. Start with the heaviest layer—often kokum syrup, jaggery, or pulp.
2. Hold a spoon just above the base and slowly pour the next layer.
3. Sip gently or serve with a straw so every layer speaks in order.

Signature Examples

- *Sunset Spritz*: Deep pink kokum, clear vodka, lime, and soda—layered like dusk on the Konkan coast
- *Golden Bloom*: Turmeric gin + orange juice + a honey foam top. Glows like a morning temple bell
- *Mango Cloud*: Mango pulp + spiced rum + coconut foam + saffron dust. A Holi celebration in a coupe glass

Fat-Washing: The Nawabi Secret

This is luxury distilled. Fat-washing is how you turn ghee, butter, or oil into an aroma, a memory, and a mouthfeel—without the grease.

Madira Mantra: Fat carries flavour. Use it to coat your spirit, not your palate.

How to

- Melt ghee, butter, or coconut oil and mix it into the spirit.
- Let it rest for a few hours and freeze. The fat rises and solidifies.
- Strain, bottle, and wait for the velvet.

Signature Sips

- *Ghee Espresso Martini*: Ghee-washed coffee liqueur shaken cold with filter coffee and jaggery
- *Butter-Rum Old-Fashioned*: Aged rum meets nutty warmth, softened with date syrup
- *Coconut Whiskey Sour*: Tropical. Toasted. Tremendously smooth

Smoked Cocktails: Where Fire Meets Fragrance

Smoke is story. One whiff and you are back at a bonfire, a temple, a winter wedding. Done right, it's not just a garnish—its memory served warm.

Madira Mantra: Let the smoke enter last, but linger longest.

How to

- Burn spices like cinnamon, clove, or even dried tulsi.
- Use charred ingredients like orange peel or betel leaf.
- Capture smoke in the glass or shaker and seal.

Signature Examples

- *Charred Negroni*: Betel-washed gin, Campari, vermouth, served in a smoke-kissed glass
- *Honey Smoked Toddy*: A winter warmer with burnt honey, whiskey, clove
- *Burnt Cinnamon Monk*: Classic Old Monk rum with fire-touched cinnamon and jaggery

Infusions and Tinctures: The Alchemy of Patience

Infusions are how herbs, fruits, and spices leave their whisper in your drink. Tinctures are their louder cousins—fast, intense, and often unexpected.

Madira Mantra: Let ingredients steep in silence. Good things take days.

How to Make

- Add dried or fresh ingredients to spirit.
- Store in glass, out of sunlight, then shake occasionally.
- Taste after 2-5 days and strain. Store. Serve with intention.

Ideas

- *Spiced Gin*: Fennel seeds, dried ginger, and betel leaf
- *Hibiscus Tequila*: Floral, tart, and pink as a Pushkar sky
- *Mango Vodka*: Soaked with ripe mango and the promise of May

Final Sip: The Future of Indian Cocktails

Technique is tradition in evolution.

In the hands of a mindful maker, even the most modern cocktail becomes a tribute to the past.

Let your drinks be bold. Let them be slow. Let them be you.

And let every glass carry not just flavour—but philosophy.

This is *Madira*. This is the new Indian cocktail.

Stir it. Smoke it. Sip it. Remember it.

Appendix C: The Cocktail Guestbook

Your Personal Mixology Journal

A great cocktail book doesn't just teach—it inspires creativity. Every reader, every home bartender, every cocktail enthusiast has their own journey, and this section is yours to fill.

This is not just a book—it's a conversation between you and your cocktails.

How to Use This Section

1. Experiment and Record Your Creations

Tried a recipe and made a small tweak? Maybe you swapped **kokum for tamarind**, or replaced **honey with jaggery**? Write it down! The best cocktails are born from experimentation.

- **Cocktail Name 1:** ______________________
- **Base Spirit:** ______________________
- **Key Ingredients and Infusions:** ______________________
- **Tweak You Made:** ______________________
- **Taste Notes and Rating (1-5 Stars):** ______________________
- **Cocktail Name 2:** ______________________
- **Base Spirit:** ______________________
- **Key Ingredients and Infusions:** ______________________

- **Tweak You Made:** ______________________
- **Taste Notes and Rating (1-5 Stars):** ______________

2. Your Personal Flavour Profile: Know What You Love

Every drinker has their own preference. Some love bold, spirit-forward cocktails, while others prefer light, refreshing spritzers. Over time, you'll start recognizing the ingredients you love the most.

Mark your favourite Indian ingredients below:

- Gondhoraj Lime
- Kokum
- Jaggery Syrup
- Tulsi (Holy Basil)
- Betel Leaf
- Saffron
- Raw Mango
- Tamarind
- Kashmiri Kahwa Spices
- Others:

____

Now, the next time you make a cocktail, you'll know **exactly what to reach for.**

3. Rate and Tweak the Book's Recipes

Love a recipe but feel like it needs a little something extra? Maybe you want to dial up the spice or tone down the sweetness. This is your space to keep track of your preferences and adjustments.

- **Recipe Name:** ______________________
- **Original Rating (1-5 Stars):** ______________

- **Tweak You Made:** ______
- **Final Rating after the Tweak:** ______

Every mixologist has a signature touch—this is where you define yours.

4. Your Signature Cocktail: Make It and Name It!

Every great bartender has a drink they are known for. Whether you love citrusy spritzers or deep, smoky drinks, your unique cocktail deserves to be written down.

- **Name of Your Signature Cocktail:** ______
- **What Inspired It?** ______
- **Flavour Profile (Light, Spiced, Bold, Herbal, Fruity, etc.):** ______
- **Key Ingredients:** ______
- **Mixing Method (Shaken, Stirred, Muddled, etc.):** ______
- **Best Served in:** ______
- **Best Paired with (Food, Mood, or Occasion):** ______
- **Final Notes and Refinements:** ______

Who knows? Maybe this will be the next classic cocktail everyone talks about!

Final Words: This Is Your Story, Your Book, Your Bar

Cocktails are more than drinks in a glass—they are memories in the making. This space is yours to experiment, refine, and track your journey into the world of mixology.

So, grab a pen, jot down your thoughts, and make this book your own.

Your perfect cocktail is just a few experiments away!

Appendix D: India's Spirit Landscape: Regions That Shape Our Cocktails

Courtesy: The Good Craft Co., Diageo India

A Glossary of Indigenous Indian Spirits

These aren't just drinks.

They are forests you can sip. Songs you can pour.

Each one carries a fingerprint of the land it rose from—fermented in clay, whispered through rituals, stirred with memory.

In a world obsessed with imports and labels, these spirits remind us that India was never lacking. Just overlooked.

What follows is a tribute—a quiet honouring—of the alcohols that survived colonization, stigma, and silence.

They are bold, fragrant, untamed.

Arrack

Origin: South India and Sri Lanka

What It Is: A strong spirit distilled from coconut flower sap or rice. Traditionally made in coastal villages and temple towns, Arrack was a drink of both festivity and faith.

Cultural Note: Once celebrated in royal kitchens and village feasts alike, Arrack was served with reverence. Its smoky depth made it a staple in rituals and moonlit storytelling circles.

Flavour Profile: Rustic, smoky, tropical; with notes of toasted rice, charred coconut, and faint spice.

In Cocktails: Often used in ceremonial concoctions and festival punches. Arrack brings gravitas to herbal mixes, earthy sours, and jungle-inspired highballs.

Legacy: Marginalized during colonial rule in favour of Western spirits, Arrack is now experiencing a quiet renaissance in India's craft cocktail movement.

Feni

Origin: Goa

What It Is: A sharp, fruity distillate made from cashew apple or coconut sap, depending on the season and the region.

Cultural Note: Feni was long relegated to beach shacks and tourist stereotypes, yet it remained a Goan staple—sipped after meals, poured at weddings, and revered during cashew harvests.

Flavour Profile: Funky, fruity, bold; with raw tropical sweetness, earthy undertones, and a punchy nose.

In Cocktails: Perfect in chai-spiced sours, peppery spritzes, or with kokum-laced bitters. Feni thrives when treated as a protagonist.

Legacy: Once misunderstood and mocked, feni now holds GI status and is being barrel-aged, blended, and boldly celebrated by Indian and global bartenders alike.

Kallu (Toddy in Telugu and Southern traditions)

Origin: Andhra Pradesh, Telangana, and parts of Tamil Nadu and Kerala

What It Is: The fermented version of neera—naturally alcoholic, cloudy-white, and full of effervescence. Tapped from palm inflorescences and left to ferment for several hours.

Cultural Note: Kallu is deeply woven into community rituals—shared during labour celebrations, funerals, and everyday respite. It's handled with quiet respect, a symbol of both simplicity and resilience.

Flavour Profile: Sour-sweet, slightly effervescent, with notes of fermenting fruit, wet earth, and forest floor.

In Cocktails: Often used in rustic coolers or smoky jungle-inspired mixes. Traditionally poured from clay pots, Kallu adds depth to citrusy profiles and balances intense spices.

Legacy: Once dismissed as 'poor man's liquor,' Kallu is now reclaiming its place in the mixology movement as a storyteller's spirit, raw and poetic.

Mahua

Origin: Central India (Chhattisgarh, Madhya Pradesh, Odisha)

What It Is: A floral spirit distilled from the nectar of mahua flowers, traditionally fermented in earthenware and copper.

Cultural Note: In tribal households, Mahua was more than a drink—it was sacred. It signified life, survival, and sovereignty. Passed down by matriarchs, it was offered to gods before it touched the lips of mortals.

Flavour Profile: Nutty, honeyed, earthy; with floral high notes and a soft, bitter tail.

In Cocktails: Used in warm toddies, honey sours, or infused with forest botanicals. mahua pairs beautifully with jaggery, tamarind, or turmeric.

Legacy: Once banned, stigmatized, and erased from menus, Mahua is finally being bottled with dignity and recognized as India's first official heritage spirit.

Neera

Origin: Maharashtra, Karnataka, Andhra Pradesh, Tamil Nadu

What It Is: The non-alcoholic, fresh morning sap of various palm species—tapped at dawn before fermentation begins.

Cultural Note: Often consumed warm with jaggery and cardamom, Neera is seen as a nourishing, cooling tonic in Indian Ayurveda and village tradition. It was a breakfast ritual before the day began.

Flavour Profile: Refreshingly sweet, floral, and clean—like drinking sunlight filtered through a palm leaf.

In Cocktails: Served warm with saffron and spice or chilled with lime and honey. It's a beautiful base for comfort cocktails or mindful mixers.

Legacy: Often eclipsed by its fermented cousin Kallu, Neera is now being reclaimed as a wellness-forward, poetic ingredient in both modern and ancestral beverages.

Rice Beer (*Handia*, *Apong*, *Zutho*, *Chhang*, etc.)

Origin: Jharkhand, Assam, Nagaland, Ladakh, and tribal belts across Central and Northeast India

What It Is: A fermented beverage made from rice and indigenous herbs or yeast cakes, often brewed by hand in homes.

Cultural Note: Brewed by women and passed between generations, rice beer is a staple at childbirths, harvest festivals, and ancestral offerings. It is poured in bamboo mugs and served with song.

Flavour Profile: Light, sour-sweet, fermented; with grainy notes and a gentle effervescence.

In Cocktails: Works well in earthy smashes, monsoon-inspired cocktails, or low-alcohol blends with tamarind and chilli.

Legacy: Once confined to tribal kitchens and dismissed by urban palates, rice beer is emerging as a slow-drinking symbol of indigenous resilience and craft.

Toddy (also see: Kallu/Neera)

Origin: Coastal India (Kerala, Tamil Nadu, Andhra Pradesh, Goa)

What It Is: A naturally fermented palm sap, similar to Kallu, often tapped from coconut or date palms and lightly alcoholic.

Cultural Note: Toddy is often sold in roadside shacks and consumed by fishermen at day's end. In folklore and kitchens, it's both livelihood and legacy.

Flavour Profile: Mildly sweet, lightly fermented, with hints of citrus, sap, and summer heat.

In Cocktails: Toddy's gentle fizz and sap-like sweetness work well in tropical highballs, sour bases, or when combined with toasted spice syrups.

Legacy: Long seen as a working man's drink, toddy is now being crafted, cold-bottled, and slowly reintroduced into thoughtful mixology narratives.

A Glossary of Ingredients and Rituals

The Language of Madira

Every drink in this book holds more than just liquid—it holds memory, landscape, and tradition. This glossary gathers the most cherished elements of Indian mixology, not as textbook terms, but as sensory stories.

INGREDIENTS—from Earth to Elixir

Arrack

A bold, ancient spirit from rice or coconut sap. Smoky, spirited, and historic.

Bael

Wood apple with healing bitterness. Used in syrups, sodas, and summer stillness.

Bhang

Cannabis leaves blended into thandai. Intoxicating in ritual and rich in folklore.

Cardamom

Minty-sweet and floral. Crushed, infused, or flamed—always aromatic.

Cinnamon

Warming, woody, and subtle. Used in spiced syrups or smoked into cocktails.

Clove

Fiery and fragrant. Just one bud can perfume a winter drink.

Cumin

Toasted for earthiness, it anchors citrusy or tangy cocktails.

Feni

A cashew or coconut distillate from Goa. Funky, unapologetic, and deeply coastal.

Ginger

Sharp, warm, and zingy. Used in syrups, smashes, and winter punches.

Gondhoraj Lime

Fragrant Bengali citrus. More aroma than acid. A lime that perfumes the room.

Jaggery

Unrefined cane sugar. Molasses-rich and earthy. The soul of Indian sweetness.

Jamun

The Indian blackberry. Tart, tannic, and tinted in nostalgia.

Kala Namak (Black Salt)

Sulfuric, funky volcanic salt. Adds digestive charm and rebellious edge.

Kokum

A deep red souring fruit from the Konkan coast. Cooling and complex.

Mahua

A tribal forest flower distilled into spirit. Floral, wild, and once sacred. India in its most forgotten form.

Orgeat

A sweet almond syrup. Creamy and nostalgic. Sometimes spiced with cardamom or saffron.

Paan

Betel leaf. A flavour bomb of herbal depth. Often tinctured or used as garnish.

Pepper

Spicy and bold. Crushed or infused for edge and warmth.

Rose Syrup

Made from Damask petals. Floral memory in syrup form.

Saffron

Golden thread of royalty. Infuses warmth, luxury, and sunset hue.

Sandalwood

Fragrant wood infusion. Sacred, cooling, and subtly smoky.

Thandai
A spiced milk blend with almonds, fennel, rose, and saffron. Served at Holi. Sacred and playful.

Toddy
Tapped from palm trees and naturally fermented. Rustic sweetness and a whisper of rebellion.

Tulsi
Sacred basil. Herbal, grounding, and often flame-kissed into spirits.

Vetiver
Aromatic root used in ancient cooling drinks. Earthy, grounding, and spiritual.

TECHNIQUES—From Ritual to Reinvention

Charred
A technique to flame-kiss ingredients like peels or herbs. Adds drama and smoke.

Clarification
Milk-washing a drink to make it crystal clear. Removes harshness, keeps soul.

Dehydration
Dried fruits and peels used as garnish. Preserved beauty.

Fat-Washing
Infusing butter, ghee, or coconut oil into spirits. Adds body, warmth, and luxury.

Fermentation

Naturally bubbling drinks from fruit and sugar. Soft fizz, old magic.

Foam

Airy cap made from aquafaba or egg white. A cloud of aroma and elegance.

Infusion

Slow-steeping of herbs, spices, or fruit into spirits or syrups. Memory captured in liquid.

Reduction

Simmering ingredients into bold syrups. Thick with intent.

Shrub

Vinegar-based syrup made with fruits and sugar. Bright, tart, and shelf-stable.

Smoke

Infusing drinks or glasses with fire or burnt aromatics. Elemental and evocative.

Tincture

A concentrated extract. Often just a drop, but potent in presence.

ELEMENTS—What India Adds to Every Glass

Aam Panna

Raw mango cooler. Tangy, nostalgic, and always refreshing.

Camphor

Used in sacred rituals. Rarely used, but sometimes tinctured for its spiritual intensity.

Gulkand

Rose petal preserve. Lush, sticky, and dessert-like.

Nannari Syrup

Made from sarsaparilla root. Sweet, fragrant, and cooling.

Saffron

Listed again here for its elemental power—both luxury and light.

Thandai

Also listed above, but in elemental form, this is Holi's official potion of memory.

The Cultural Glossary of Madira

What Shapes Our Sips

Every cocktail in *Madira* carries more than flavour. It carries centuries of meaning—rituals, symbols, seasons, and subtle cues. This cultural glossary captures the emotional grammar of Indian drinking.

Aarti

A circular offering of flame to the divine. The original bar ritual, where hands moved in rhythm and light crowned the offering.

Barse

A baby's naming ceremony. Marked by saffron milk, almond thandai, and sweetened first sips of identity.

Charpai

A woven rope cot. Found in courtyards and under trees. A place where toddy, time, and storytelling unfold.

Daana

A sacred act of giving. Grain, fruit, or liquor offered in spirit and humility.

Desi

Of the soil. Of the people. Whether a spirit or a spice, 'desi' roots it to the land.

Garam Taseer

Warming in nature. Used to describe ingredients like saffron, clove, or nutmeg that heat from within.

Ghar Ka Nuskha

Home remedy. Recipes passed by whisper and memory. Where most Indian drinks begin.

Grishma Ritu

The summer season. When mangoes ripen, kokum cools, and drinks must soothe.

Holi

The festival of colours and intoxication. Bhang, thandai, and laughter in the sun.

Itihas

History. Every cocktail in *Madira* nods to it—not just with ingredients, but with intention.

Kalash

A ceremonial vessel filled with water, mango leaves, and coconut. Symbol of purity and abundance.

Kansa

A bronze alloy used for utensils. When spirits are sipped from kansa tumblers, they carry earth and elegance.

Matka

Earthen pot used for storing water or brewing toddy. Keeps the spirit grounded and cool.

Mehekti Yaadein

Fragrant memories. The kind left behind by a rose syrup or sandalwood drink.

Meetha

Sweet. But in Indian drinks, sweetness is never just sugar—it's mood, comfort, affection.

Nostalgia

A recurring ingredient in *Madira*. Found in rose milk, nimbu pani, or a quiet sip under neem shade.

Odiyan

Traditional village brewer and spirit keeper. Knows the jungle, the moon, and the right mix.

Panchamrit

A sacred mix of milk, curd, honey, sugar, and ghee. The first five-ingredient cocktail.

Puja

A sacred ritual of offering. Drinks served during puja are for gratitude, not intoxication.

Rasa

The emotional essence of taste—joy, sorrow, peace, surprise. What your tongue remembers long after.

Ritual

The hidden architecture of Indian life. Every stir, strain, or garnish in *Madira* nods to it.

Saatvik

Pure, balanced, and calming. Often non-alcoholic, but spiritually potent.

Sabr

Patience. What every good infusion, fermentation, or reduction demands.

Samskara

A rite of passage. From first sips at weddings to last toasts at farewell feasts.

Sharbat

Flavoured syrups and waters offered to guests. The Indian welcome drink.

Shraddha

A ritual of remembrance. Ancestors are offered water, rice, and sometimes, a quiet dram.

Thali

The Indian meal platter. Drinks often sit quietly in its corner, balancing spice and serving memory.

Utsav

Celebration. The very reason most drinks in *Madira* exist.

Viraha

Longing. A mood best captured in slow-sipped negronis or night-time toddies.

Rupa

85

03/4/26